Living Christianity

Living Christianity

A PASTORAL THEOLOGY FOR TODAY

Shannon Craigo-Snell

and

Shawnthea Monroe

Fortress Press

Minneapolis

LIVING CHRISTIANITY
A Pastoral Theology for Today

Cover photo: © Glow Images / SuperStock
Cover design: Laurie Ingram
Book design: PerfecType, Nashville, TN

Library of Congress Cataloging-in-Publication Data

Craigo-Snell, Shannon Nichole.
  Living Christianity : a pastoral theology for today / Shannon Craigo-Snell and Shawnthea Monroe.
      p. cm.
  Includes bibliographical references and index.
  ISBN 978-0-8006-6381-0 (alk. paper)
  1. Theology, Practical. 2. Christian life. 3. Theology, Doctrinal. I. Monroe, Shawnthea. II. Title.
  BV3.C73 2009
  230—dc22
                              2009006093

The paper used in this publication meets the minimum requirements of American National Standard for Information Sciences—Permanence of Paper for Printed Library Materials, ANSI Z329.48-1984.
Manufactured in the U.S.A.

Contents

Preface

Staying in Touch

This book is intended to give the reader an opportunity to see what happens at the crossroad of the theological academy and the parish.

We two authors met in divinity school, back in the salad days, when the future was a limitless horizon of possibility. It was there we both fell in love with theology, enjoying the luxury of being students, able to immerse ourselves in this new language until we were fluent enough to join the conversation. We found that it was possible for theology to be reflexive, a dialogue of give-and-take between the needs of the church and the demands of doctrine. These conversations about theology were inspiring; and as we moved into distinct professional lives, we assumed they would continue.

After graduation, we discovered the ugly truth: real life in the church and in the academy is a far cry from the fantasy we'd imagined in seminary. It turns out there are many forces that pull pastors and professors in different directions. Pastors are consumed with the tasks of ministry, serving as preacher, teacher, administrator, counselor, and (if necessary) janitor. Theological study and reflection often give way to more pressing issues, like recruiting Sunday school teachers or balancing the budget. When a pastor manages to carve out a moment for study and reflection, she discovers that academic theology is rarely written in an inviting and accessible way. Out of school, we pastors can lose our facility with theological language, and the categories and issues become fuzzy.

The academic's life has its own obstacles and challenges. Professors are often consumed with committee work, efforts to meet the needs of students, and the ongoing task of keeping current in the field while also participating in a high-level intellectual discussion of contemporary theology. Furthermore, when it comes to publications, attending to the needs of the church isn't necessarily rewarded professionally.

Luckily, the bonds of friendship kept us from losing touch with one another, despite our different vocational demands. Now, fifteen years later, the ongoing theological conversation between a pastor and a professor has become part of our everyday lives. And while we are far from the idyllic place we imagined in seminary, we've discovered that there is something essential and life-giving to be gained when pastors and professors discuss theology.

This book is not a constructive systematic theology—a new and comprehensive account of the doctrines of Christianity. Nor is it a pastor's reference book that will provide quick resources on how to navigate specific difficulties within a congregation. And it is definitely not a self-help book for pastors, professors, or Christians in general. Instead, it is an example of what can happen when academic theology and pastoral experience intersect and engage one another. Our objective in writing this book is to invite others—pastors, professors, and laity—to join in the conversation.

Even in writing this book, we have different aims. Shawnthea, the senior minister of a United Church of Christ (UCC) church, hopes to model how a pastor can act as a translator between academic theology and the everyday realities of Christian life. As a pastor, she speaks both languages. She can hear in the intellectual discourse of theology the insights that offer real resources to her parishioners and then communicate these insights pastorally so they can be heard and incorporated into a life of faith. At the same time, she can identify the theological issues just beneath the surface in everyday congregational activities, articulate what is at stake, and pose these pressing questions to theologians. Shawnthea aims to do this work of translation in a way that does not lessen the rigor of theology or simplify the messy reality that is the life of the church.

Shannon, a theology professor, wants to model a practice of bringing the history and framework of systematic theology to bear on issues that confront Christians today. She sifts through the historical developments of doctrine, the conceptual frameworks of Christian beliefs, and the current situations in which Christians find themselves in hopes of identifying pertinent connections among them. As a teacher, Shannon strives to encourage and equip her students to think carefully, creatively, and critically about the roles Christianity plays in our contemporary world, broadly understood. This includes how the ideas and customs of Christianity function in political discussions, what visions of God are implicitly operative in American consumer culture, how thoughtful congregations could communally discern faithful responses to social injustice, and what shapes Christian engagement with the world.

These goals may sound lofty, but they really boil down to getting thoughtful people to talk about the real issues that arise in the course of living as Christians, and to do so with as many theological resources as we can garner. In the chapters that follow, we address specific Christian doctrines, offer resources, and make connections between academic theology and church life—all with an eye toward bringing the two closer together.

The reader will note that we speak in two distinct voices. Shannon speaks as an academic, offering information, ideas, questions, and ways of thinking about each topic. Shawnthea speaks as a pastor, reflecting carefully on the ways that these topics play out and influence the lives of people in her congregation. Shannon uses longer words; Shawnthea tells better stories.

Shannon's work complicates things. She rejects simplistic answers, emphasizes the multiplicity of Christian beliefs and practices, and underlines the historical specificity of different ways of thinking. To someone looking for the one answer, Shannon offers many answers, new questions, and reasons to be suspicious of singular approaches.

Shawnthea does not simplify things. Rather, what she does is show how an awareness of theological complexity can nurture a faith that is resilient, supple, and coherent. She demonstrates that complexity is not confusion and models the pastoral effectiveness of a rich and nuanced understanding of Christianity.

A Word to Theologians from Shannon

This kind of dialogue is valuable to theologians who are committed to Christian faith and to the church for three reasons. First, the questions we ask are vital to the communities to which we hold ourselves accountable. The second reason has to do with the very nature of Christian theology. Christian theology is not the philosophical belief system of an individual believer, plucked from the atmosphere or discerned through mathematical equations. Christian theology is a kind of knowledge that is communally held, generated, and performed in and through the life of concrete Christian churches. Attempts to separate out formulaic beliefs or reduce the rich complexity of how Christian communities know into a straightforward philosophical system diminish the thick reality of

Christian theology into a thin sliver of thought. Trying to make sharp distinctions between what Christians think about God and how they worship together, act in the world, teach their children, and so on results in a woefully incomplete view. Thus the very knowledge that Christian theologians seek cannot be found apart from the life of the church. It makes sense, then, not only to participate in the church but also to talk about theology with ministers and parishioners.

The third reason this kind of conversation is valuable for theologians concerns the pervasive influence of Christian theology. Christianity influences much of our shared world, including contemporary political, economic, military, and social realities. Yet often our public discussions about these aspects of life do not inquire into the roles Christianity plays or do not answer such inquiries adequately. This means that many people who study these various issues miss part of what is really·going on because they overlook the influence of Christianity or fail to grasp its complexity. It also means that many Christians are never invited or challenged to bring their faith to bear on their understanding of the rest of the world. In public discourse, Christian voices are most often heard on only a handful of hot-button issues labeled as religious, such as abortion, homosexuality, or creationism. Then the discussion tends to stagnate at a very low level, so that only one Christian perspective is heard and the theological and pastoral complexities of the issue are completely avoided. Many other issues that are deeply theological and relevant to Christians (such as immigration, health care, social security reform, etc.) are rarely addressed in a public forum from perspectives of faith. Because of all of this, there has been a growing recognition in recent years that America needs more public theologians. We need theologians who can help analyze public events theologically, raise the level of public discourse about religion in general and Christianity in particular, and encourage all Christians to think carefully and critically about the engagement between faith and public life. There have been influential intellectual public theologians in the past, such as Reinhold Niebuhr, Martin Luther King Jr., and Karl Rahner. Yet today there is a lack of this kind of theological engagement.

Theologian Rosemary Carbine argues that the first step toward doing public theology is to create a public, that is to help foster a community that can engage in that kind of discourse.[1] If we want a higher level of theological conversation to happen in the public forum in America, we need to provide resources to help people engage in such conversation. This means offering, in an accessible form, at least an introduction to the history, conceptual framework, and language of theology. Conversation between pastors, theologians, and laity can be very beneficial to theologians in helping to create an informed and engaged public in which public theology can happen.

One further note. Up to this point I have used the term *theologians* to refer to professional academics who teach and write theology. Yet one of the goals of my own work—in teaching, writing, and this book in particular—is to encourage many people to engage in the work of theology: to talk about God, to question how visions of God shape our communities, and to wrestle with the issue of how the holy and the human interact. As leaders of communities of faith who daily articulate understandings of God, pastors are already knee-deep in the work of theology. Anyone can be a theologian; pastors must be theologians.

A Word to Pastors from Shawnthea

Let's face it. Theology is like a foreign language to most pastors—we learn it in school but quickly lose our facility for it when we don't use it. But the truth is that if you can learn to understand contemporary issues in theological terms, you can bring two thousand years of wisdom to bear on real-life problems. The Christian tradition thus becomes a remarkable resource for meeting the challenges of modern life. Having a more robust understanding of theology also allows pastors to identify what is at stake in the life of the church and the various issues that arise. Personally, it is easier for me to determine which battles are worth fighting and which small changes will have large impacts if I can see what theological issues underlie the day-to-day challenges that emerge in parish life.

Yet the best thing about ongoing theological engagement is that it produces a consistent faith, which enables a pastor to respond to questions, concerns, or events in the moment. A well-developed theology gives rise to a sort of theological instinct, so that off-the-cuff responses, daily decisions, and unconscious attitudes all express a coherent, thoughtful, and faithful view of God.

I would also add that laypeople benefit as well, for if pastors can teach parishioners how to think theologically, they can begin to see their everyday lives as the realm of God's ongoing activity. Thus equipped, Christians are able to enter into the theological conversation on their own.

The Structure of This Text

In each of the chapters of this book, we address a particular topic in Christian theology that we think is important today. Shannon offers theological frameworks and resources for addressing this topic, as well as introducing some tools and concepts that are crucial for theological inquiry. Shawnthea explores how these theological structures and ideas might play out in the life of the church.

Chapter 1 focuses on creation. Shannon interprets current debates about creationism and evolution as deeply intertwined with how Christians understand the Bible and what we are looking for in this text. She suspects that people who occupy the extreme positions in this debate (in which a literal reading of the Bible rejects any kind of evolution, or in which evolutionary science rejects any kind of creation) share a common desire for certainty that is a characteristic of the modern period in the West. The question then arises, is certainty what the Bible offers or what Christianity is about? The resources offered in this chapter include brief descriptions of modernity and postmodernity, as well as a discussion of biblical interpretation. Shawnthea then translates these resources into a sermon on the creation texts of Genesis, pastorally shaping the questions of what kind of knowledge the Bible offers us and how it informs a life of faith.

Chapter 2 addresses Christology, exploring the many ways in which Christians in different times and places have understood the affirmation that Jesus saves. Here Shannon introduces the rich history of this doctrine as well as the academic discipline of systematic theology. She describes how different Christian communities have located the salvific power of Jesus in different moments within the narrative of his birth, life, death, and resurrection. Shawnthea then reflects on how such theological commitments play out in congregations. To do this, she describes two fictional but familiar churches that understand the saving work of Jesus differently. One emphasizes his life and ministry, while the other highlights the power of the resurrection. For each church, Shawnthea traces the many ways Christology can be expressed in and shaped by everything from the worship space, to the hymns sung, to the ministry to the world.

In chapter 3 Shannon describes a portion of this history and addresses some of the differences between Roman Catholic and Reformed Protestant perspectives on the doctrine of sin. She also discusses liberation theologies and the remarkable influence they have had on understandings of sin in the past decades as they have offered new ways to interpret the communal nature of human sinfulness. Identifying some of the benefits of a sturdy doctrine of sin, Shannon argues that this doctrine can be a countercultural force against American consumerism. This is followed by a constructive argument concerning the inward focus of the doctrine of sin, offered by Shannon and Shawnthea together. The chapter concludes with a sermon in which Shawnthea uses a robust doctrine of sin to proclaim the good news.

Chapter 4 looks at ecclesiology, the doctrine of the church. Here Shawnthea engages the work of theologian Karl Barth, exploring his view of the church and articulating how it helps her shape her own congregational commitments. Shannon then models the process of constructive theology, engaging the work of Peter Brook, who is not a Christian theologian but rather a theatre director. Looking at the church through the lens of Brook's analysis of theatre allows Shannon creatively to engage the tradition while reinterpreting it in a contemporary light and emphasizing the communal and embodied characteristics of Christianity.

Finally, chapter 5 addresses the topic of heaven. While up to this point the conversation has been between Shawnthea and Shannon, here it is extended outward, answering specific questions of Christian laypeople. This is an embodiment of what the entire book is intended to be—an invitation to join in the conversation. Throughout our responses, we continue to tease out of these questions what is at stake both theologically and pastorally.

Acknowledgments

From Shannon: I am deeply grateful to the many people who have supported and encouraged the writing of this book. The Louisville Institute provided funding for our collaboration, without which this project would have remained a fantasy. David and Julie Kelsey encouraged me to pursue this nontraditional format, and David offered critical feedback throughout the writing process. Marilyn McCord Adams read the entire manuscript and provided comments that greatly improved the text. Other friends and colleagues, including Beth and Mel Keiser, Stephen Davis, Ludger Viefhues-Bailey, Bill Goettler, Adrian Cerezo, Camille Lizarribar, Amy Laura Hall, and Cynthia Hess, read portions of the manuscript. Their insights made the best parts of this text better and prevented many errors and mistakes. Scott Larson provided brilliant assistance with the manuscript and valuable theological conversation. For the time to write this book, I thank my husband, Seth Craigo-Snell, and the community in which we are raising our children, which includes Matt and Jill Bracksieck, Kathy and Jack McMurray, Abiyoyo, the Davis family, and the Viefhues-Bailey family. The space to write this book was given by Oshel and Joanna Craigo, who offered us a bit of heaven on the Gulf Coast. My portions of this book, as well as my desire to write it, grew out of my teaching. I am extremely grateful to the students I have worked with over the years, who have taught me so much and made living in New Haven worth the tribulation that is February. I am also grateful to the wonderful teachers I have learned from in my life, whose examples provide daily inspiration. Finally, I must thank Shawnthea, but I do not know any words adequate to the task. Her friendship is one of the greatest blessings in my life.

This book is dedicated to my children—Jacob, Elias, and Lucy—whose thoughtful questions daily require me to speak of God with honesty, humility, and simplicity, and to my parents—Oshel and Joanna—who instilled in me a love of education.

From Shawnthea: We began this project five children, five degrees, and five jobs ago. It would not have come to completion if it were not for a "great cloud of witnesses" who encouraged, counseled, and challenged us. Among the witnesses, I want to thank the Joneses: Vivian, the Welshman who introduced me to Jesus Christ, and Serene, the Oklahoman who introduced me to Karl Barth. I'm grateful also for the friendship and guidance of faithful preachers—like David Bartlett, Barbara Lundblad, and Tom Long—who make the hard work of turning scripture, theology, and real life into good news seem effortless. Jim Nieman, Verity Jones, and Clyde Steckel deserve medals for reading working drafts of the manuscript, letting us know where the gaps were. In addition, this book couldn't have been written without the support and forbearance of the dear people of First Congregational Church (Moorhead, Minnesota) and Plymouth Church of Shaker Heights (Ohio), who have received my ministry, warts and all, with grace. As always, I'm grateful for my husband, Neil Mueller, and my children, Walter, Clara, and Ren, who endured my absences and my deadlines. I also want to thank the Louisville Institute, whose commitment to inviting academics and pastors to the same table has changed the conversation for the better. Most of all, though, I give thanks to God for Shannon Craigo-Snell, a woman of valor whose loyal friendship and razor-sharp intelligence have made me a better person. "Give her a share of the fruit of her hands and let her works praise her in the city gates" (Prov. 31:31).

I dedicate this book to Helen Virginia Monroe, who taught me to think for myself, and to Grace Sherwood Monroe, who taught me to believe.

One

Creation

God and Certainty
Shannon Craigo-Snell

Theology or Epistemology?

The Christian doctrine of creation has been enjoying the limelight
lately. Newspapers report school board battles over teaching evolution in schools; newsmagazines rehash conversations about the
relationship between science and faith. Unfortunately, while the
media are paying attention to the topic of creation, they are not
paying attention to the actual theology of creation. The debate
around evolution and creationism is not about the doctrine of creation, but primarily about how we know things, or epistemology.[1]
School boards engage in brouhahas over the teaching of evolution,
but actually they are grappling with questions of how we know the
world around us. Do we know about the world through science,
religion, or both?

Many scientists and science-appreciating people simply view science and religion as two separate ways of knowing. Science is the way of knowing that should be taught in science class in a public school in a country that separates church and state. Religion is the way of knowing that should be taught in religious institutions and families. People who feel this way are not necessarily negating religious views of creation, but they believe that such views are not science. They do not fall within the purview of a discipline devoted to explanations of the natural order.

Similarly, many Christians find no problem believing both that God created the world and that Darwin was probably right about the process of evolution. They can imagine that the workings of evolution are part of God's creative process. Next to the challenge of believing that Jesus is both fully God and fully human, or that God is both one and three, holding together creation and evolution doesn't seem that difficult.

However, some Christians find a deep incompatibility between the biblical account of creation and a Darwinian depiction of the world evolving into its present state. Some reject the immense age of the universe implied in the evolutionary view, believing that the Bible presents a much younger world. Some cherish the notion that God created each type of animal with its current features intact and bristle at the thought that major characteristics of animals (including humans) have changed significantly over time. And some view the theory of evolution as an explanation of how we came to be that writes God out of the picture, reducing humanity to a product of random chance in a world that is not ultimately ordered by the love of God, but rather is an outgrowth of biological processes with no greater purpose than species survival. For some Christians who see evolution and creation as incompatible, the theory of evolution veils a picture of the universe unhinged from any greater meaning than what we can manage to scrape out of our own lives day by day.

Biblical Accounts of Creation

Often these various concerns are anchored to the idea that evolution contradicts the accounts of creation offered in Genesis. Creationists want a more literal reading of the biblical text. Looking closely at the creation stories in Genesis, however, raises questions about whether a literal reading is appropriate. There are two stories of creation in Genesis, which seem to have been formed in different contexts and with different aims.[2]

In the first story, God creates through a series of declamations ("Let there be light!"). Biblical scholars think this narrative was formed during the Babylonian exile, when the Hebrew people were struggling to understand their faith and its similarities to and differences from the beliefs of people around them.[3] The shape of the story follows the same pattern as a Babylonian creation tale, the *Enuma Elish*. The similarity of structure makes the differences stand out quite clearly. The primary difference is that the *Enuma Elish* depicts the world as arising from a divine dispute between two deities. Marduk kills Tiamat, and her slain body becomes the universe.[4] The blood of her consort, Kingu, is mixed with clay to form humankind, a race intended to serve the deities.[5] In stark contrast, this first creation story in the book of Genesis makes it very clear that the universe is not the result of an argument between multiple gods, but is created intentionally by the one almighty God.[6] Humankind is not a race of servants, but a race of creatures made in the image of God.[7]

The second biblical story of creation includes the creation of humanity from the earth and the account of Adam and Eve's exile from the Garden of Eden. This is thought to be a combination of two previously existing stories. This narrative describes and accounts for the ambiguity of creation—for both the profound goodness of creation and the painful realities of sin and evil, for both the nearness of God and the distance of God.[8]

As is the case with many other biblical texts, it is difficult to read these stories literally. Like the stories of Saul becoming king and of Jesus' birth, these creation stories offer more than one account of what happened, and they cannot be neatly merged into one factual report of historical events or scientific processes. Such multiplicity poses the question: How can both accounts be true? The answer: Both can be true if one understands these stories to be neither science nor history.

Modern Confrontations

In his influential book *The Eclipse of Biblical Narrative*, Christian theologian Hans Frei argues that the nineteenth century saw a major shift in how Christians interpreted the Bible. Prior to that time, he contends, Christians understood the Bible to be the major overarching truth of the world into which all other accounts of reality fit. The biblical narrative was the lens through which all other information was viewed. The Bible was seen as a supple, abundant text that could be interpreted in various overlapping ways. It could be read literally, allegorically, typologically, and so on.[9] This rich text contained more meaning than could possibly be gained by any one person, method, or even generation.

Then changes began to happen in the West. Beginning in the seventeenth century, throughout the early modern period and the Enlightenment, deep shifts occurred in epistemology, in the understanding of how we know things. Rationality came to the fore as the primary—perhaps the only—legitimate way of knowing. Modern science was seen as a clear path to objective knowledge, and factual accuracy became the indispensable measure of truth.

These developments had significant influence on how the Bible was read and interpreted. The Bible moved from being the overarching truth into which all other forms of truth fit into being merely one source of truth within a worldview dominated by rationality and historicity. It was a tremendous paradigm shift: instead of seeing the world through the lens of the Bible, Christians began to see the Bible through the lens of the world.[10] People began asking—often and seriously—if the stories in the Bible were reasonable, factual, and historically accurate. Some people attempted to discredit Christianity by pointing out ways in which biblical narratives apparently fall short of these standards.

Many Christians sought to defend the Bible. Some did so by arguing that the biblical stories *are* reasonable, factual, and accurate—that they do meet the standards of modern reason, science, and history. Others did so by arguing that the Bible is not history or science, but myth. As myth, the Bible conveys universal truths, truths that ultimately reside outside the text, and therefore are untouched by scientific and historic challenges.

Focusing on developments of the nineteenth century, Frei argues that these methods of defending Christianity were more dangerous than the attack. Recognizing the narrative structure of much of the Bible—the structure that is "eclipsed" by reading the Bible as history or myth—is critical to unlocking the supple meanings of the text. In narrative, the meaning of the text is inseparable from the stories themselves. The meaning cannot be conveyed just as well by another historical account of the same events or by another myth with the same moral. Rather, the meaning of narrative is inextricably bound to these particular stories. Frei contends that it is wrongheaded to defend the Bible as accurate history or admirable myth. Such defenses flatten and distort not only the meaning of the Bible for Christians, but the way in which the Bible *creates meaning*, because narrative meaning is more multilayered, evocative, contextual, and communal than historical knowledge or universal morals learned from myths.

We can see something of this in a mundane example. My mother tells a story of how I came to her crying when I was five years old. I had just heard the story of Adam and Eve in the garden for the first time. I was devastated by the idea that Eve had disobeyed God, confused by the idea that the good creation got spoiled, and scared of a snake that could speak. While some sort of conversation like this surely happened, my mother does not tell this story to accurately and objectively recount a past event. She tells it to illustrate that I was always interested in theology and to simultaneously brag about my precocious questioning and complain about what she had to put up with in raising a theologically inquisitive child. Her telling of it and my hearing form part of our current relationship and can be most fully understood in the context of that relationship.

Our stories convey multiple meanings on many levels all at once. The stories of the Bible do likewise, only exponentially more so. If our own family stories are shaped to relate more than one truth at a time, surely the stories of the Bible are further saturated with meaning, with layers of truth that can be accessed through different methods of interpretation and different experiential perspectives.

Seen in light of Frei's analysis, arguments that declare the historical and scientific accuracy of the biblical creation narratives look like attempts to reduce the rich text of the Bible to the level of a lab report. Such arguments make science, in which procedures are noted exactly, the standard by which the Bible is judged. They overlook the many pliable and subtle ways in which these stories convey meaning, focusing on one form of meaning that fits neither the time nor the genre of these texts.

This problem is exacerbated by the current generation of creationists, those who talk of intelligent design. Like many savvy conservatives, proponents of intelligent design intend to put forth their argument in terms that are unimpeachable by secular standards. So they leave out all mention of God and the Bible, speaking instead of teaching a diversity of views and fostering debate and critical examination of theories. They attempt to argue on scientific grounds that Darwin's theory has holes. More specifically, they claim that creatures exhibit characteristics that cannot be explained with the logic of evolution.[11] They then assert that these characteristics, and the universe as a whole, are better accounted for by the idea that the cosmos is the product of an (unidentified) intelligent designer. The trouble is, there is no clear science behind these assertions. Furthermore, these claims betray the methodological naturalism to which science as a discipline is committed. This is not science; it is creationism reworked.

Not all Christians who oppose evolution support intelligent design. Some Christians who reject evolution also reject attempts to push intelligent design into public schools. They say the battle is lost when Christians stop talking about God, leaving the designer unidentified.

I say the battle was first invented, then surrendered, when proponents of intelligent design decided that science was the lens through which to view the Bible. It is not a science book. There are many excellent science textbooks available. None of them comes close to containing and engendering as much meaning as the Bible. None evokes my devotion, guides my life, or shapes the questions of my existence.

Why do people do this? Why do they fight the tough battle of convincing Americans that the Bible is a science book when it is so much more? One important reason concerns epistemology. Proponents of intelligent design have, on some level, bought into the modern mind-set that science provides the kind of meaning that matters most. Therefore, if the Bible is to retain its significance, it must offer science. More specifically, it must offer certainty.

The Modern Quest for Certainty

The modern era has been marked by a quest for certainty, a hope of finding secure knowledge to anchor human endeavors in a confusing world.[12] Scholars pinpoint the beginning of the modern era at different points in time. I like to point to a writing by Descartes called *Discourse on Method*. In this deceptively slim volume, Descartes lays out the underpinnings of the modern preoccupation with epistemology. He wrote at a time when Europe had been plagued by multiple wars, many related to religious issues; when frightening climatic changes had decreased crop yields and seriously affected human life; when scientific discoveries in many different fields had shattered stable worldviews and opened up whole new ways of looking at the world; when increasing cultural diversity and religious pluralism confronted Christians with the challenges of different perspectives. In the midst of this confusion, Descartes recognized that his view of the world would have been quite different had he been born in another culture. His example is this: the same man would be quite different were he raised in Europe or among "the cannibals."[13] Descartes was aware that his own social location and upbringing had profoundly shaped his view of the world around him and that the same was true for other people. Many of the disagreements that lead to conflict and warfare could be avoided, he hoped, if people could peel away the influence of culture in order to get to the basic truths on which we can all agree.

We can recognize this logic. In a time of warfare, don't we all think that surely, as reasonable people with some bare minimum of common sense, we ought to be able to figure out a better way to settle disputes than this? Can't we tap into our common humanity, start with what we do agree on, and go from there?

In the turbulent context of the seventeenth century, Descartes wanted to find a firm foundation for human knowledge. He wanted to find some baseline or touchstone that all human beings could agree on, that would cut across cultural dividing lines and form the basis of peaceful human relations. Descartes was confronted with a confusing and dangerous world, and he wanted to find some bit of certainty to hang on to, to build on. This desire was fueled by the beginning of modern science, which was just starting to offer the enticing possibility of objective knowledge, which would be demonstrably true for any person, anywhere, regardless of culture. In *Discourse on Method*, Descartes pursues the two related goals of finding the firm foundation of human knowledge and of providing an account of the emerging scientific methodology.

The most famous passage in the book is when Descartes decides that to find such a sturdy foundation, he must first raze the flawed construction of cultural beliefs that muddy his thinking. He decides that to find the certain truth, he must first doubt everything. He sits in front of a fire and attempts to doubt all things. He finds that there is one thing he cannot doubt—his own thinking: "I think, therefore I am."[14]

This is arguably the beginning of modernity, which is not really a time period but rather a worldview. The modern worldview is a way of thinking that we in the West are familiar with because it still prevails today. It is centered on the human person, seen first as an autonomous, rational individual. It privileges the mind over the body, asserting that a person can peel away the layers of influence of her or his particular physical, social, and cultural location to get to the unhindered truth. It claims that there is value in rigorously questioning all of our assumptions. It believes that if we all think clearly enough, rationally enough, we will all reach the same conclusions. It exalts reason as the primary characteristic of humanity. Underneath all of this there is a belief in a singular, stable Truth that we can find if we think well enough.[15] So the task is to find it, to find that certain truth and hold on tight.

We are, in many ways, in a similar situation to that of Descartes. There are wars around the globe, increasing bloodshed tied to religious commitments. Climate change is affecting us, with more devastating events, such as hurricanes and mudslides, and a frightening outlook. Diversity and pluralism continue to challenge us daily, and we escape through nostalgic fictions of a unified past. So many of us, like Descartes, are looking for certainty. There are Christians who want the Bible to be that pure touchstone of knowledge, who want the creationist certainty of knowing that the world is made according to God's exact specifications, part of a divine plan and under divine control. Likewise, there is a minority report among science buffs who look to further scientific research to disprove God's existence, or at least provide the scientific explanation for the human need to invent God.[16] Such persons look to science for the certainty of cause, effect, and explanation, for predictable outcomes and the exclusion of what is beyond human knowledge. In some ways these polar opposites are actually two sides of the same coin—both groups are continuing the profoundly modern quest for certain knowledge.

Postmodern Questioning

If modernity is a particular way of seeing the world instead of a time period, then it does not end on a given date when a new era begins. Instead, there is a shift in worldviews that happens slowly as the old perspective becomes less persuasive and a new perspective becomes dominant. Whether we are now seeing the demise of modernity, or are perhaps still in modernity's early stages, is a decision that will have to be made far in the future. However, it is clear that the basic tenets of modernity have come under attack from several quarters. Many of the criticisms can be loosely grouped together under the umbrella term *postmodernism.*

While much of the lingo of postmodernism is confusing and off-putting, the basic sense of what it is about is fairly straight-forward. Postmodernism is a sustained critique of modernity that is taking place in many different fields, from philosophy and religious studies to theatre, art, and architecture. This critique is not something wholly new and different from modernity. It is the logical outgrowth and radicalization of modernity itself. Recall Descartes's understanding that culture shapes how we know the world and his determination to doubt everything he thought he knew. He believed he could peel away the layers of cultural influence, present in his own assumptions, to get to the firm knowledge of reason. Postmodernism takes Descartes's own project further by doubting the assumptions Descartes himself missed. If good thinking requires questioning all assumptions, then eventually the assumptions of modernity come into question. Postmodernism, then, is the exposing and questioning of unacknowledged assumptions behind modernity.[17]

So a postmodernist might point out that Descartes did not question everything. He did not question his belief that there is a universal human reason beneath cultural influence or his idea that if we all could think clearly enough, we would agree. He assumed that layers of cultural influence *could* be peeled away and that doing so would reveal a firm center of Truth.

Perhaps, such a postmodernist might suggest, we can keep peeling layers forever because there is no core. Maybe we cannot peel them at all, because that would require that we step out of our own skin. Descartes assumed we could step out of our own cultural location long enough to see which parts of our worldview are culturally inherited and which parts are grounded in reason. Maybe we cannot do that.

Postmodern critiques take many forms and cannot be reduced to a single attack on modernity or a single intellectual standpoint.

This is why *postmodernism* is an umbrella term that covers many different ideas, theories, and authors. One idea that is used in many forms of postmodernism is that of social construction. This idea has roots in the early modern period. The Enlightenment emphasis on education stemmed from a recognition that training could deeply influence a person. Descartes himself understood that his own upbringing profoundly shaped his view of the world, as illustrated in his remarks about cannibalism.

Postmodernism takes this modern insight further, looking closely at how social location and experience shape how we know, how we behave, and who we are. Various postmodern scholars suggest that knowledge is socially constructed (such as the knowledge that cannibalism is wrong), that gender is socially constructed (girls learn to be feminine in response to cultural expectations), and that the human person is socially constructed (I come to be myself in relation to other people over time). Again, none of these points is unique to postmodernism—each has its roots in modernity—but postmodernism develops them all.

The idea of social construction relies on seeing human beings as communal and social. We learn how to think and act in a community, which has practices and institutions set up to teach us how to think and act. Many ideas and ways of life that we think of as simply normal or natural, or that we don't even think of at all but just take for granted, are actually things that we learn in community. Those practices and institutions are also things that are created by the community over time. There are cycles of communal meaning-making that form us, that socially construct much of our reality.

Some of these cycles are deeply destructive. Examples from the early modern period include the horrors of slavery and the oppression of women. Since modernity defines humans as primarily rational, the more rational someone is, the more human he or she is. Conversely, people associated more with the body than with the mind, such as mothers and enslaved African Americans, were seen as less rational and less human. Since they were viewed as less rational, women and African Americans were understood to be suited to work related to the body and, therefore, to need less education. The lack of education and restriction to bodily work furthered the appearance of deficient rationality. It is impossible to determine where the circle starts—there is no answer to the chicken-egg question. But it is possible to see how human cultural conventions become so entrenched that the reality that they are human conventions is forgotten. Instead, they are seen as givens, as natural. Then they may be defended on those very grounds. It is unnatural for women to spend their days reading and writing! Postmodernism exposes such cycles, pointing out the ways in which human cultures create meanings then forget that such meanings are the products of their own creation.

Some postmodern authors take social construction quite far, asserting that there is no meaning that has not been constructed by human communities over time. Other postmodernists take a more moderate view. If there is a core of meaning that is not socially constructed, we have to acknowledge that our access to it is socially constructed. The way that we perceive, interpret, act on, and value any core knowledge will be profoundly influenced by the social construction of our realities. My way of knowing the world has been so profoundly formed by my particular culture that I will see everything—no matter how different—through that lens.[18]

While there is a spectrum of postmodern positions on the depth of social construction, most of them are still quite threatening to a desire for scientific certainty about God. Even the more moderate views demand that we grapple with the difficulty of knowing about God through texts written and interpreted by humans, through experiences shaped by cultural patterns and norms, and through traditions created by human communities. While moderate post-modern views acknowledge that there may well be a God outside of human social construction, they also challenge us to recognize that all knowledge of God is enabled and limited by our socially constructed ways of knowing.

A more extreme postmodern position would be that God is socially constructed. Again, like many things postmodern, this idea is not new, but rather has strong roots in modernity. One clear root to this idea is the work of Ludwig Feuerbach, a nineteenth-century philosopher who offered one of the first "projection" theories of religion. The basic idea is that humanity projects its highest hopes and aspirations for human goodness and meaning onto the sky, creating an image of the Holy that then serves to inspire and guide human beings. For Feuerbach, this was not an antireligious idea; rather, it was an affirmation of the Holy and the Divine, which he understood to be the communally sanctified human desire for good. Others, such as Sigmund Freud, have used similar projection theories to dismiss religion altogether or to understand it as a negative phenomenon. Among postmodernists who consider God a social construction, a similar diversity of views is evident. Some are faithful Christians who believe that human beings create the Holy through ritual, prayer, kindness, and love. A cathedral can be a sacred space not because God somehow shows up there, but because generations of believing Christians have met there to pray, to imagine a better world, to tend the needs of others, and to affirm the importance of beauty. Others believe that humans have created a false God and forgotten that this God is our own creation.

Modernity asks, how do we cast the influence of culture aside so we can get to what is given, the Truth above and beneath human culture? Strong forms of postmodernity ask, what if what you think is given is actually something created? What if our creating goes further and further down, perhaps infinitely so? What if there is no Truth with a capital *T*, but rather just endless layers of human production of meaning, various interpretations without a stable anchor or divine arbiter?

This type of postmodern questioning thrives on college campuses and in urban coffee shops. Yet its influence has expanded and is felt in much of mainstream American culture. The idea of social construction is persuasive, and many postmodern questions follow logically from it. Books and films have been showing these ideas in different forms—from Faulkner novels to Matrix movies—for decades. At the same time, the pluralism and diversity of the contemporary world influence our daily lives—lives that often feel fragmented, disjointed, and profoundly uncertain. Many people who could not begin to define the term *postmodern* nonetheless experience and understand the questions postmodernism raises. While we still are surrounded by the modern worldview, it is not as reassuring as it once was.

Faith and the Doctrine of Creation

I suspect that the creeping onslaught of postmodernism has something to do with the current liveliness of the creationism debate. We are facing many challenges similar to those Descartes encountered, only ours come in more extreme postmodern forms. In response, some people on both sides of the creationism debate demand—as Descartes did—human certainty. Some choose the certainty of relentless cause and effect without room for mystery or miracle; others choose the certainty of biblical stories as accurate historical, scientific data that cannot be questioned. For many of us, however, these are unattractive options.

Theory, history, and theology all give us reasons to be wary of the quest for certainty. Postmodernism (and its many modern precursors) has taught us that social construction shapes how we know. Globalization helps us to recognize, as travel did for Descartes, that location and culture deeply influence how we see the world. Theory thus reveals that the certainty of human knowledge is often an illusion. Furthermore, we have seen how the bright shining ideals of modernity—liberty, equality, and brotherhood—have often come to ruin when groups were certain that their view, and no other, was correct. History teaches us that absolute certainty about one's own knowledge often accompanies oppression of those who see the world differently. From both theory and history, we have learned to value a bit of epistemic humility. We have learned that it is wise not to grasp too tightly for certainty, not to imagine that we know it all.

Theology can also speak to this issue in a number of different ways. From such thinkers as Hans Frei (and many others), Christians can learn to think carefully before allowing the modern, secular world to set the terms of the debate. The modern period is marked by an obsession with epistemology—with figuring out precisely how and what humans know. This spotlight on epistemology leaves many things shadowed and out of view. When this light is directed at Christianity, the fullness of Christian faith is reduced to a particular way of knowing. All of the rituals, practices, service, ethics, communion, and community that are an enormous part of Christianity go unseen. If Christians view our own tradition through the lens of modern epistemology—with its passion for certainty—we see only a thin, dim, and listless reflection of ourselves.

Faith looks quite different when it is understood in terms of Christian theology rather than modern epistemology. From a theological viewpoint, faith is not a second-best form of scientific certainty, or even a superior form of the same, but rather an upwelling of trust within relationships of love. Faith does not attempt to reduce the mystery of God to a factual statement that can be comprehended by the human mind. Faith is embodied, enacted, communal, and performative. Faith is life lived out of, and into, the abundant meaning that God grants to human life.

As Christian faith is not merely a way of knowing, the doctrine of creation is not a foundation on which to build a stronghold of modern certainty. It is neither an antidote for postmodern pluralism and fragmentation nor an escape route out of the diverse and confusing realm of contemporary intellectual conversation. Instead of offering certainty, the doctrine of creation provides rich resources for understanding what it means to be human in relationship with God and with the world around us. These resources begin with the biblical stories and with the comforting, challenging assertions these stories hold.

In our lives we encounter mind-boggling goodness and heart-rending evil. The doctrine of creation reminds us that as destructive and painful as this world truly is, it is also deeply, profoundly, and primarily good. Without negating the reality of pain and suffering, the Christian doctrine of creation assures us that the universe is good and—despite abundant evidence to the contrary!—so are we. I personally find this to be the most challenging claim in all of Christian theology. What kind of goodness can be attributed to all of creation, including humanity? Is creation aesthetically good, morally good, or simply intrinsically valuable? While I believe much of creation is good in these ways, there is too much suffering, cruelty, and waste in the world for me to easily ascribe these kinds of goodness to the whole cosmos. Thus for me, the goodness of creation, from which stems its beauty, morality, and value, is a theological affirmation based on the provenance of creation, as attested to in the biblical texts. The cosmos is good because it is created by God, declared good by God and ordained to eternal goodness with God.

The doctrine of creation also assures us that the universe is not an accident. It is not a product of chance or the by-product of an argument between beings more powerful than ourselves. Creation is the handiwork of a loving and powerful God. Much of the world as we know it came to be through long, slow processes, both biological and cultural. But the meaning of the world exceeds human culture and human knowledge. The world is held within a larger matrix of meaning; it rests within the arms of a loving God.

We live in a moment when the meaning that humanity has been making of creation is quite frightening. We have brought the earth to the brink of nuclear disaster, are in the midst of raging ecological destruction, and face stark predictions of climatic nightmares in the future. In this context the affirmation that the meaning of creation is not entirely constructed by human culture does not mean we are off the hook. Tilting between modernity and postmodernity, our theological reflections on creation must reckon with our own meaning-making power while acknowledging (gratefully) that not all meaning is produced by humanity. God creates the universe, loves and delights in it. The meaning that we make of and in this creation ought to honor and reflect this divine provenance. Creation is a gift from God; it is grace, and the proper human response should include humility and gratitude.

It is important to recognize what theological work the doctrine of creation does and does not do. The theological content of the Christian doctrine of creation does not offer Cartesian certainty to stave off the confusion of diversity, the perils of religious warfare, and the dread of climate change. Instead, basic theological affirmations, rooted in the biblical accounts of creation, provide a framework for rich reflections on how Christian faith—in all its dimensions—lives the relationship between humanity, cosmos, and Creator.

One further comment regarding the crucial but limited scope of the doctrine of creation: The most thoughtful reservations about evolution that I have ever heard come from undergraduate students. If creation happens through evolution, it is a long process in which the future is a product of the past. This worries some of my students, who hear in the gospel the possibility of something truly new, of a future that is not just the outgrowth of the past. These students worry that when Christians accept that creation could happen through evolution, we give up believing in a God who can interrupt this linear progression with transformative grace. They want to believe that God continues to introduce miraculous and new realities—that such divine power was not limited to the first instant of the cosmos.

Let me be clear that these students are not desperate for specific reenactments of biblical miracles. Rational, modern intellectuals, they are not expecting the blind to suddenly see or the loaves to multiply. Rather, they recognize the possibility of transformation—personal, communal, and even cosmological—as central to the good news. The promise that the future can be something other than what has been prepared and produced by the past is a vital element of Christianity. Sinners can be saved; the oppressed can be liberated; cycles of abuse can be stopped; swords can be beaten into plowshares. All of this happens by the grace of a God whose power is not bounded by the linear unfolding of past into present into future.

To these insightful students, I offer another reminder about the limits of the theological work of the doctrine of creation. Christian theology does not speak of God only as Creator. Were every drop of theological wisdom to be wrung completely out of this doctrine, such that we knew everything we could of God the Creator, we still would not know the fullness of God. God is also Jesus Christ and Holy Spirit. Christian assertions that God is triune demand that we describe God in three different ways. If we ask the doctrine of creation to account for all of who God is, we inadvertently diminish the importance of Jesus and the Spirit, imagining that the truth of God could be told without mentioning them.

I think my students are right. Understanding God as creating through evolution does neglect the redemptive and transformative powers of the Divine. However, we cannot end the conversation about God with creation. We must also speak of Jesus the Redeemer and of the transformative Spirit of God.

"The Why Chromosome": Genesis 1
Shawnthea Monroe

In our local newspaper, a fiery debate is taking place in the letters to the editor. What is generating so much heat? Not property taxes or zoning laws. Not local economic development and not even war. No, the issue that has pitted neighbor against neighbor is creation—or rather, creation*ism*.

A topic that generates this much passion ought to be addressed from the pulpit, I suppose, but I can't work up much enthusiasm for it. Why? I know who's in front of me. This congregation is full of smart, educated, and well-read people. Yes, we are people of faith who believe in God and who follow Jesus Christ, but we are also people who have been to school. We have studied biology and chemistry, and we are grounded in the scientific method, relying on what is provable and testable and measurable. Ask anyone here how the world was made, and we immediately think in scientific terms. We might talk about the big bang or Darwin's theory of evolution, or perhaps quote Stephen Hawking or Albert Einstein. The creationists love to quote the Bible, especially Genesis, but I doubt that anyone here would begin discussing creation by quoting Genesis. We're just not that kind of people.

In fact, when we hear that in 1999, the state of Kentucky outlawed the use of the word *evolution* in its science textbooks, we wince and wonder, "What is the world coming to?" And when we read about school boards requiring that creationism or intelligent design be taught along with evolution, as if they were equally valid scientific theories, we shake our heads at the irrationality of it all. What can you say to people who want to treat their naive readings of the Bible as if they were laboratory evidence? What can you do with people who are so . . . unreasonable?

So, no matter how hot the topic may be in the local papers, when the subject of creation or creationism comes up, I quickly lose interest in the conversation or try to change the subject. This seems to me like someone else's fight. Even though I am a pastor and view everything from the perspective of faith, I still have a rational mind and a deep respect for the merits of scientific thinking. Who wants to be baited into discussing intelligent design or creationism? Leave those conversations to the folks who handle snakes.

However, while I may not be interested in creationism, the problem with closing my ears and mind to the debate is that, in the name of being educated and rational, I may come dangerously close to banning faith talk altogether when it comes to thinking about the creation. If I did that, it would be a sign that I had allowed my own thinking to fall into the same trap as that of the creationists. I would be treating the theological idea of creation and the biological idea of evolution as two scientific theories that operate on the same plane and compete with each other. You have to choose one or the other. But are they really in competition? The creationists say they are, and the hard-core rationalists say they are. But maybe they are just different answers to the same question.

For example, if someone asks, "Why is the water boiling?" a scientist would say that if you heat water to a certain temperature, it will begin to change from a liquid state to a gaseous state, forming bubbles that rise up and dissipate into the air; hence the water boils. Stop by the church and ask the same question, "Why is the water boiling?" and I would say, "Because I want a cup of tea." Both answers are correct: one, the scientific explanation of how water boils; the other, a more human explanation of why I put the kettle on. Not every question about why the water is boiling should be answered by scientists.

In the same way, the view that God wisely created you and me and all humanity and the theory that human life evolved as a process of nature from less complex forms are not competing claims. Perhaps they are simply different answers to the question, "How did we get here?" When I look at it this way, I begin to think that even those people who champion the teaching of creationism may have a valid point because they are protesting against the steady erosion of our most deeply held values about the world and our place in it. These values are being neglected in the public sphere, and it's high time people of faith woke up to the peril.

Or perhaps these aren't different answers to the same questions—maybe the questions are different. If you listen to the first chapter of Genesis, there is no mistaking this for a science textbook. It's poetic and powerful, a wild and wonderful story, full of lush images that draw us in. It's a story that builds and builds and builds until even the voice of God is caught up in the excitement and God exclaims, "This is not just good! This is *exceedingly* good!" I don't think Genesis was ever meant to answer the question of *how* we got here. No. Genesis is answering the more important question of *why* we are here.

I'm reminded of the story of the little boy who asks his mother where he came from. Though his mother thinks it's a little early for this talk, she takes a deep breath and then offers a careful explanation of human sexual reproduction, even touching on issues of

Christian marriage and human love. When she finishes, her son stares at her for a moment and then says, "Well, I was just wondering, because Michael said he's from Detroit." Before we answer, we need to understand the question.

So if we want to know about the division of cells or the means of natural selection, a good book on the theory of evolution is what we need. But if we want to understand what it means that we are here, what it means to be human, what value we should place on this planet, and what responsibilities are ours toward it, those are different questions, and a biology textbook will be silent toward them. To inquire into these questions, our best resource is the doctrine of creation, and to understand this doctrine is the beginning of sound faith. If we understand the deep meanings of the claim that God created the heavens and the earth and all that is in them, we can begin to see who we are and where we are and our role as stewards, called to care for God's good creation. It gives us something to hold on to when we face bigger questions.

In our culture, we have come a long way in answering the question of "how." From genetics to biology to astronomy, we are discovering more and more about the world and how we got here. But the question I think we have avoided is "Why?" Why are we here? That's where Genesis begins to make sense.

Why are we here? That's the question at the heart of every creation story—and there are many. Every culture has developed its own narrative answer to the question of why, from the Epic of Gilgamesh to the Roman myth of Romulus and Remus to the tales of Wakatanka. Every great culture has a story of "in the beginning." What most of these stories have in common is that they are violent and gory, tales of destruction and chaos out of which gods and humans emerge.

But not our story. Our story is not about violence or destruction or even sex. Our story is about thought and word, spirit and love, creation and blessing. This is a story of creation in which there are no accidents. The Creator wills everything into being, and every created thing is seen fully by God, who says, "This is good. This is good. This is exceedingly good." And at the very apex of God's creative project, we arrive, bearing the image of the one who breathed life into us.

So why are we here? There are many faithful answers to this question, but I think Genesis hints at a powerful one. Picture it: God was creating out of void and nothingness, speaking into being the stars and sun, sea and sky, and everything was good. Then God stopped speaking, entered into this creation, getting down and dirty, laid hands on the newly formed soil, and made humankind. With the first holy breath of life, we became the ultimate hybrid, born of matter and spirit, ground and glory. Yes, we are one of the creatures, but we come bearing the image of God.

Maybe that's why we are here. We were created to be in a conscious relationship with the living God and the living world. Perhaps God wanted someone to work with, someone who could participate in this holy and good project.

Yet if we take this role as "cocreators" seriously, there is good news and bad news. The good news is that we are good. That's one of the hardest concepts for people to accept these days, that we are actually good. During the week, part of my ministry is a ministry of presence. People knock on my door seeking a place to set down their burdens. They're disappointed, they're hurt, they're lost, they've made serious mistakes, sinning against God and against the ones they love. But what they all have in common is that down deep, they don't believe they are good. They all believe that somehow what they've done or who they are has made them unworthy and undeserving of the love and respect of family and friends and coworkers. And they certainly don't deserve the love of God.

So I turn to Genesis and assure them, as I assure you, as I assure myself, that created by God, we are good. Full stop. Whatever else may happen, however we use our gifts, however we choose to behave—or misbehave—we are good. And nothing and no one can take that away from us, for it has been determined and declared by the Lord. We are good, and we've been blessed.

The bad news is that we may be good, but we're also responsible. We are responsible. Yes, we are good and have a blessing within us, but we must take responsibility for ourselves—for what we do and for how we act in this world.

In Genesis when God set humankind in the world and said, "I give you dominion over all this," it wasn't carte blanche to use creation to fulfill our own selfish desires or to live without any regard for what happens to the rest of the world. No, God was saying, "I trust you enough to make you responsible."

We're responsible, not just for ourselves, but for the whole of creation. (And I thought taking care of pets was tough!) We have a creation to watch over, and so far we're not doing very well. Time doesn't permit me to list all the troubling signs in nature that indicate our global environment is under stress. We know about global warming, we know about the growing hole in the ozone, we know the storm systems are changing and becoming more powerful and violent. Things are changing, and not for the better. I find it all depressing and overwhelming; it makes me want to hide under the bed in my air-conditioned house.

But we can't hide. Because we are part of creation and God has called us to be not just creatures but stewards, this is news that should not just pass through us or by us—this is news *for* us. As Christians, we need a vibrant and robust understanding of creation so we can get some traction on these critical issues. Much will have to change, not just for our children, but starting with us—right here, right now. We will have to change the way we work, the way we play, the way we live. These choices are beyond our capacity for sacrifice if we continue to believe environmental issues are simply issues of science. They aren't—they are issues of faith.

Genesis is a story of love and relationship, a story that tells us that we are here because God decided to put us here, that God loves us and has judged us good, and that God expects us to be responsible for this beautiful creation in which we find ourselves. As we face the growing crisis of the changing global environment and deal with the hard choices that have to be made, there is one more piece of news: We are not alone. God didn't breathe life into humankind and say, "Good luck! I'll see you at the end!" No. God is with us, still speaking, still acting, still present.

This news is somewhat mixed, isn't it? It's like a friend of mine whose son went through a terrible adolescence. He was always getting into trouble, always testing the limits, making bad choices. All his mother could do was hold him accountable and wait for him to wise up. She enforced every rule and made good on all the consequences, which made her son furious. In the middle of one particularly bad time in his life, he shouted, "I won't play by your rules! I don't love you! Why don't you just leave me alone?" She looked at her son and said, "Honey, I have good news and I have bad news. The good news is that I love you and I'm sticking around. The bad news is . . . I love you and I'm sticking around." And so is God.

God is still here, still holding us accountable to that original blessing and responsibility, assuring us that we are loved, that we are good, but we have work to do.

Two

Christ

Jesus Saves
Shannon Craigo-Snell

I grew up in small-town West Virginia in a time when it was assumed that everyone was Christian. Denominational quarrels aside, there was a sense that Christianity was one thing, that we all knew what it was, and that—while we might argue about some of the details—we all agreed on the major points. Driving through the breathtaking beauty of the Appalachian Mountains, it is not uncommon to see three wooden crosses erected by the side of the road, or even to see the statement "Jesus saves" painted on an overpass. The challenge is that this apparently unanimous agreement that "Jesus saves" masks both the mystery and the history of this statement.

This two-word declaration—"Jesus saves"—opens up into a million questions. How does Jesus save? What part of Jesus' life and works is salvific—which bit does the trick? Is it his birth? Death? Resurrection? What does Jesus save us from? Sin? Finitude? Death?

Damnation? Do we really all need saving? Does the Jesus event change God's attitude toward us? Our attitude toward God? Both?

How someone answers these questions about Jesus, about Christology, influences everything else she or he can say in theology. It shapes theological claims about how best to worship God and how to live a Christian life, about what came before us in creation and what comes next in the new creation. These topics are deeply interconnected, and Jesus is right in the middle of them all. Theological statements about how Jesus saves have implications (that is, make implicit claims) for creation, revelation, the human person, sin, the Trinity, heaven and hell, and every other theological topic. These issues are so intertwined, it can be difficult to see where one stops and another starts, or even how to begin to talk about Jesus. The issues are like a bowl of fishhooks—you intend to pick up just one, but you get the whole jumble in your hand. So how do we start to talk about Jesus, just Jesus, while recognizing that Christology is connected to everything else in theology?

That particular task is the specialty of a discipline called systematic theology—the practice of taking Christian doctrines apart, one by one, in order to understand how they are related to one another.

Systematics and Scrunchies

My understanding of systematic theology is shaped by a night I spent in an orphanage in Guatemala several years ago. The orphanage was organized into distinct homes, each with a house mother and several children of various ages. I was welcomed into one such home by a handful of cheerful and energetic young girls, around six to ten years old. I was surprised by the girls' defiant happiness and humbled by their hospitality. Not long after arriving, I noticed that all of the girls wore scrunchies in their hair. A scrunchie is a stretchy circle of fabric that is used to pull long hair into a pony-tail. More decorative than rubber bands or regular hair elastics, scrunchies became popular in the 1980s here in the States. Each girl seemed to have one and to be proud of this possession. One of the older girls seemed particularly smart and sassy, and she explained how they got these scrunchies over the course of the evening.

This girl had been given a scrunchie made of yarn, woven into a pattern that gave it a certain amount of stretchiness. It was a hand-me-down and a treasure, something useful and beautiful and her own. But this gift came with a problem. What to do with one scrunchie in a house full of eight long-haired girls? Should she keep it for herself? Should they share the scrunchie, taking turns?

Instead of these options, the young girl decided to take the scrunchie apart. She bravely took scissors to her prized possession and cut through every thread. Very carefully, she unwove the mate-rial, paying close attention to the pattern of the weaving in order to learn how to weave her own scrunchie. She found that if she wove the yarn just right, the strands would hold together, would give enough to be put around her hair, and would spring back enough to hold a ponytail. She then rewove her original scrunchie, wove others for her housemates, and taught her friends how to weave still more. Clearly the girls had improvised on the original pattern, making scrunchies in new colors and new designs.

My brief stay at the orphanage was part of a travel seminar to Central America, which in turn was part of a larger course of study focused on liberation theologies. I was in the midst of train-ing to become a professional theologian at the time, and the trip shaped my theology in many ways. In particular, these girls with their scrunchies became my model for the task and discipline of systematic theology.

In this book, we are talking about the God of Christianity by separating out particular topics and discussing them individually. This way of doing things places us within the tradition of systematic theology. Theology is simply talk about God. More fully, it is the communication of a whole thought about God—not random insight, but a sense of how the whole picture of God and the world holds together. Systematic theology is a particular way of talking about God that separates various topics within the Christian story and treats them separately in order to see clearly how they connect with one another. The theological claims of systematics are made both in the particular things said in regard to each doctrine and by the overall organization of those doctrines.

For many people, systematic theology can be off-putting. To some, it seems to arbitrarily conform to old patterns of thought, limiting the scope of theological questions and answers. It can seem to be more concerned with philosophical coherence and academic rigor than with the lived vitality of Christian faith. The discipline of systematic theology can appear overly rigid, unimaginative, and traditional in the deadliest sense of the word. It is a pattern of discourse that, until recent years, has been shaped almost exclusively by men of privilege, and in modern history it has been dominated by white European and American men. Thus many women and people of color choose not to engage in systematics. When it is seen in this light, to speak the language of systematic theology is to speak in the patterns of white men, to ask and answer questions set by someone else. If systematic theology is the norm, then the unique insights of women and people of color are missed, and their voices are allowed into the conversation only insofar as they follow, engage, or illumine white male patterns of discourse. From this perspective, it is important that systematic theology not be seen as the most important or primary form of Christian theology.

Yet seen from another perspective, systematic theology is like the work of the young girl at the orphanage. It is the process of taking apart the theology of a given community to see how it is put together. It is learning how to weave your own theology. Systematic theology carefully unweaves the strands of theology so they can be rewoven in new patterns while still holding coherently together.

Good theology should be much like the scrunchies the young Guatemalan girls made. It should have enough give to gather together, enough strength to hold. It should be functional as well as beautiful. It should be made in a community that learns and weaves together, and it should—delightfully—vary with each individual. Good theology should do work for a Christian in her daily life, holding back long hair so she can concentrate on the task at hand; and it should comfort her, reminding her that she is dearly loved, even in the moments when she feels like a motherless child.

In this view, the different doctrines are not old-fashioned topics that can't make room for new ideas, but rather elements of the Christian story that provide resources for addressing any issue in the life of the congregation. We can generate them from the Christian narrative. They include God, creation, human person, sin, incarnation, person of Christ, work of Christ, cross, resurrection, justification, sanctification, Holy Spirit, church, Scripture, sacraments, and eschatology. Each of these is a thread of the Christian narrative and Christian life. They are woven together, such that if you pull one thread, it shifts and moves each of the others.

In the scrunchie-weaving task of systematics, the organization of topics also conveys theological meaning. For example, where do we put revelation in this list? Does it come right after creation, since all of creation sings the glory of God? Does it come in with Jesus? Does it come first, since anything said about theology should begin with revelation? Each of these possible choices has ripple effects. If revelation is closely linked with creation, is Jesus less important?

If revelation doesn't get addressed until Jesus is on the scene, what does this imply about Judaism and other religions? If revelation comes first, it will probably have to be quickly followed by theological anthropology, to describe the human person who receives revelation. If the human person comes before creation, do we end up with a human-centered world, shaping any of our later comments on creation? Systematic theology makes clear that every choice we make about a particular theological subject influences what we are able to say—and still be coherent—about every other topic.

Every Doctrine Has a History

Christians have been thinking about each of these topics, or doctrines, for many generations. The rich text of the Bible does not deliver crystal-clear, unequivocal statements about how to understand each aspect of the Christian story. Instead, it provides multiple narratives, evocative poetry, unsettling prophecy, and a compelling depiction of Jesus Christ. It does not give easy answers, but rather invites the reader into a long, ongoing relationship of revelation and discernment with the God of mystery and love. Thus many of the specifics of Christian traditions—from belief in the Trinity to the number of sacraments to patterns of worship—have been worked out in Christian communities, guided by the Holy Spirit, over time. Each doctrine, then, has its own history.

The history of the doctrine of Christology is marked by two major councils that attempted to guide future thought about Jesus among Christians. The First Council of Nicea, held in 325, dealt mainly with the controversial views of Arius regarding the relationship between God the Father and God the Son. Arius noted that Christians consider Jesus Christ to be God, to be the one in whom and through whom all things were made, and yet also consider Jesus to be subordinate and obedient to God the Father. Advocating a strong monotheism, Arius claimed that Jesus Christ, the Logos, was a creature. The Arian slogan "There was when he was not" denied the divinity of Christ. The response to this challenge, represented by Athanasius and endorsed by the Council of Nicea, was the assertion that Christ is *homoousios*—of one substance—with the Father. This simultaneously affirms the divinity of Christ and the Trinitarian view of God as both three and one.

In 451 the Council of Chalcedon further nuanced Christian understandings of the divinity of Christ. This council, knee-deep in multiple, complex debates, resulted in a statement that Christ is "one person in two natures." This means that Christ is both truly human and truly divine—not God masquerading as human, or two persons in one form, or some mixture of human and divine. According to Chalcedon, in the one person of Jesus Christ, there are two natures—human and divine—"which are united unconfusedly, unchangeably, indivisibly, and inseparably."[1]

The two councils deal with the twin mysteries at the heart of Christianity. God is both three and one; Jesus is both human and divine. They are not mysteries in the sense of things we have not figured out yet, unexplained phenomena, or undiscovered country. Instead, they are mysteries in the true sense of the word, aspects of the mystery of God that human minds can never comprehend. These are mysterious not because of our limited intellects and experiences, but because of God's infinite glory.

The Councils of Nicea and Chalcedon do not offer explicit descriptions of Jesus or precise formulations of salvation through Christ. What they do, instead, is refuse to break the tensions in the paradoxes. God is one and three. Easy exits from this perplexing mystery, such as considering Jesus less than God, will not do. Jesus is both fully human and fully divine. Attempts to escape that scandal by reducing his divinity, denying his humanity, or mixing or dividing them are diversions from the heart of Christian faith.

Nicea and Chalcedon do not offer a specific Christology. What they do is challenge all Christian theology to uphold the mystery of Jesus Christ.

Teaching Christology

In many churches in the United States, the claims made by Nicea and Chalcedon are well known even if the names of the councils are not. Although they may question or disagree with these claims, Christians know that orthodox theology asserts that God is triune and that Jesus is fully human and fully divine. Yet there are other elements of the history of the doctrine of Christology that are less familiar and that can generate very fruitful conversation.

Several years ago I was asked to teach a six-week Bible study course on the Passion narratives at the Lenten School of Religion in Albuquerque, New Mexico. While I did my research every week, reading Bible commentaries and doing exegetical research, for the first five weeks I learned a lot more from the students than they learned from me. I am a theologian, not a biblical scholar, and most of these students had decades on me in terms of church life, spiritual development, and the thoughtful discipline of intelligent engagement with Scripture. On the sixth Sunday, however, I reverted to form and allowed myself to teach theology. It was a quick and dirty crash course in Christology, and this is how it went.

At the beginning of the session, I asked everyone to take off his or her shoes. When we talk about Jesus, we are speaking of the heart of Christianity, the mystery of our faith, and are therefore on holy ground. This had the effect of making people laugh, be somewhat aware of their bodies, and be just a bit uncomfortable. Then I asked each of them to consider how Jesus saves. What does he do that is salvific? Whom does Jesus save? What does he save them from? The students looked befuddled at these question rephrased: What were you taught as a child about how Jesus saves. When your children ask you about Jesus, what do you say that he does? Somewhere each one of us who participates in Christian community has a default answer to this question, even if it is one that we would intellectually resist or want to significantly nuance before we fully claimed it. What is the default answer you have for how Jesus saves?

We then went around the room and each person answered. The participants gave very different answers, yet we were familiar with all of them. Jesus saves everyone; Jesus saves the faithful; Jesus saves the elect. Jesus saves us from sin; Jesus saves us from death. Jesus saves us by being a sacrifice, by showing us how to love one another, by taking our punishment on himself. While none of these answers was particularly new or shocking, the effect of this simple exercise was revelatory for several students in the room. What it revealed was not the correct answer to the question "How does Jesus save?" but rather the rich multiplicity of answers abounding within Christianity.

To help them begin thinking about the multiple answers to the question of how Jesus saves, I then gave students two different ways of approaching Christology. The first was a simple time line of Jesus' life, death, and resurrection. On a chalkboard, I drew a straight line with symbols to indicate different moments in the story: a cradle for the incarnation, a chalice for the life and ministry of Jesus, a cross, an empty tomb, and an arrow pointing forward to the new creation. I explained how Christian communities and theologians, in different times and places, have located salvation at various points within the Jesus story. Some emphasize the *incarnation,* or the birth of Jesus. When the Divine becomes human, the relationship between humanity and God is changed forever. The second-century theologian Irenaeus writes that Christ "became what we are in order to enable us to become what he is."[2] Others, such as those in the social gospel movement and some liberation theologians, emphasize the *life and ministry of Jesus*. In his life of solidarity with the oppressed, of creating new communities, and of challenging unjust social structures, Jesus provides us with a model for our own behavior and a vision of right relationship with God. The *crucifixion* has been the locus of salvation for many groups over time. Indeed, the belief that this particular death was of salvific import is dominant in much of the Christian tradition. Yet even here there is a wide variety of explanations for how and why the cross matters. Still other theologies emphasize the *resurrection*. The cross was the unfortunate consequence of the life of godliness Jesus led in a fallen world. It exposes human sin and the worst that we are. But in the resurrection God has the final word, loving us despite our sin, triumphing over evil and death. Finally, some theologies emphasize *eschatology*, locating the saving work of Jesus Christ in his inauguration of the new creation, which is already present and not yet fully realized.

We discussed how all of these various views have roots in Scripture and are part of Christian liturgical traditions. We can see these views in worship practices; we can hear them in familiar hymns. All of them are part of the multifaceted tradition we inhabit, and indeed each is deeply connected to the others. This multiplicity and fluidity is a great strength of the Christian tradition. Thus it was not surprising when students did not want to choose among them. "It's the whole thing!" they declared, wanting to embrace a vision of Jesus' salvific work that honors each element of his story. There is surely much truth in this response.

Yet, I argued, simply saying yes to each of these ways of describing the saving work of Jesus Christ results in a systematic muddle. What can be said about creation, or revelation, or heaven and hell? What should guide Christian behavior now? Should Christians proselytize, work for social justice, or strive for personal and communal purity as we await the end of days? It is hard to answer these questions without a clearer picture of what, particularly, Jesus does that saves us. To support my argument, I offered the students my scrunchie metaphor for systematics. When faced with a dozen beautiful colors of yarn, it might be difficult to choose which ones will form the structure of the scrunchie that allows for its flexibility and strength. Yet if no choices are made, the strands will not cohere into something useful and beautiful. Instead, we just have pretty yarn. So one strand, or perhaps two in close connection, comes to the fore. Others will be included, woven in tension and accent. Similarly, as Christology is deeply considered, one location for salvation becomes more prominent for each community and each theologian, even as other locations—other important parts of Jesus' life with us—are held in creative tension.

Having, at least for the moment, convinced the students that this might be worth considering, I launched into the second approach I offer students for thinking about the multiple Christian understandings of the saving work of Jesus: a brief whirlwind tour of some of the historical Christologies different theologians and communities have embraced. The timeline of the Jesus event is a comprehensive framework in the sense that almost any Christology can be placed within it. In contrast, the second approach I offer is a sampling of historical views. This is not at all comprehensive; there are many Christologies that do not fit within these traditional models. Furthermore the point here is not to study any of these theologies in depth, but rather to have a sense of the variety of views and some minimal insight into how these theological positions are formulated.

I began by explaining the *ransom theory* of atonement, associated with the theologian Origen (c. 185–254). This theory sees the blood of Christ as ransom paid to the devil.[3] Humanity, in bondage to evil and sin, is saved by the ransom paid on the cross. While this view might seem less than persuasive now, it was a significant strand of the Christian tradition for hundreds of years.[4]

I followed Origen with one of the most influential Christologies in the tradition, that of Anselm of Canterbury (c. 1033–1109). Anselm rejected the idea that Satan had any rights over sinful humanity.[5] Living in feudal times, Anselm was surrounded by an ordered society in which honor and shame played a major role. Every person was due a certain amount of honor because of his or her station. The lord of the manor was due more honor than the serf who farmed the land. Furthermore, every person had certain obligations to those both above and below in the hierarchy. The serf had to work for the lord, and the lord had to provide for the serf. In this culture, if someone did not render the service owed his superior, or if someone dishonored that superior in any way, the insult had to be dealt with carefully so that the whole social order remained secure. The severity of the insult was measured first and foremost by the status of the one who was insulted. A small act of negligence, when done toward a person of high rank, was extremely serious. An insult could be dealt with in one of two ways. Either the responsible party could be punished, or he could pay satisfaction, which meant he could give the injured party something of enough value to offset the insult. The obligation to restore the social order through punishment or satisfaction fell on everyone involved, including the family of the offender. If the responsible party could not be punished or pay satisfaction, some other member of his family must do so in his place.

This complex feudal social structure is the backdrop for Anselm's famous book *Cur Deus Homo?* (Why the God-Man?). Anselm claims that humanity has dishonored God by our sinfulness. Since God is worthy of infinite honor, the insult is infinitely serious. The dictates of justice require that humanity either be infinitely punished or pay satisfaction of infinite worth. No mere human can pay an infinite debt to God. Only God could do that. Yet the person who pays satisfaction must be a member of the human family. Thus God, being merciful as well as just, sent the God-man, who can pay the debt and who is a member of the family of the offenders. The death of the innocent Jesus on the cross is the payment of satisfaction on behalf of all humanity.

Understanding Anselm's *satisfaction theory* of atonement requires learning a bit about the culture he inhabited, so it is not intuitive to Christians today. Yet the students had no trouble understanding the basic framework and recognizing that this theory continues to be influential and to subtly shape many Christian views of Jesus and the cross.

Keeping up a break-neck pace, I moved on to the next type of Christology. Thirty years after *Cur Deus Homo?* was published, the theologian Peter Abelard refuted it. Abelard rejected the idea that God could be pleased by the death of God's own innocent Son.[6] His understanding of how Jesus saves was quite different. Abelard believed that the love that Jesus Christ gave to humanity throughout his life inspires us to love in return. When Christians encounter Jesus in the Gospel narratives, they are moved by Jesus' example to become persons who love God and neighbor. Living in an extremely similar culture to that of Anselm, Abelard also drew on feudal images to understand what happened on the cross. Instead of satisfaction, however, he lights upon the knight on the field, performing dangerous feats to woo his lady-love. The cross, then, is not required by God but is a valiant act of love that Jesus performs to woo the church into loving relation. Abelard's Christology is referred to as a *moral exemplar theory.*

This theory was appealing for a number of the younger students and was certainly familiar to everyone. The next theory I described was also familiar, another view that is alive and vibrant in many Christian communities.

During the Reformation, when there was a fascination with the law, Calvin (1509–1564) wrote a complex Christology that describes Jesus as prophet, priest, and king. How Jesus saves is understood in three ways, corresponding to these roles. Among these is the idea of *substitution*. This model has many similarities to Anselm's but relies on a juridical framework instead of the feudal system of honor and shame. Calvin proposes that the punishment that would rightly fall on humanity for sin is instead borne by Jesus on the cross. While Calvin's rich Christology incorporates other models as well, this substitution theory has been picked up in various ways by Christian communities and other theologians. The twentieth-century theologian Karl Barth (1886–1968) describes God as the judge who is judged in our place, again invoking the concept of substitution within a juridical framework.

Although there are many other descriptions and theories of how Jesus saves, out of time constraints and mercy for my students, I described only one more, the *Christus Victor* model. This view has had a diverse group of proponents, including Irenaeus (second century), Martin Luther (sixteenth century), and C. S. Lewis (twentieth century).[7] As Gustaf Aulén (twentieth century) describes this model in the book *Christus Victor*, God is in battle with Satan and the forces of evil. On the cross it appears that God has been defeated in the death of Jesus Christ, yet in the resurrection we learn that this defeat was merely temporary. While evil exercises real power in the world before the new creation (the battle is real), Christians know that the devil is no match for God and that the ultimate victory belongs to God in Jesus Christ. This model is notable for its appeal in various ages and for its encouragement to name and struggle against evil in the world.[8]

By this point in the session, the students were excited, overwhelmed, and tired of hearing me talk. They were unsure if this multiplicity of ideas was unnerving, liberating, or both. They found

it truly helpful to have someone acknowledge and explain the
ety of views that they had always known but had not recognized
as really different accounts of the work of Jesus Christ. Christology
is central to Christian life, yet these intelligent, curious, well-read
churchgoers had previously not been given the frameworks and
history to help them think it through. They were delighted, and I
was surprised. We had all forgotten that our feet were bare.

I ended this session by pulling out two points I hoped the students would remember, even as the specifics of Abelard versus
Anselm were forgotten. First, as we attempt to understand mystery,
we necessarily use the tools we have at hand. Each of the theologians I described tried to understand the inexplicable mystery of
salvation in Christ. To do so, they searched for metaphors and patterns of meaning that might apply. Invariably, the metaphors and
patterns they came up with were those that were available in their
own cultures. Ransom, honor and shame, satisfaction, legal procedures, knights on the field of valor—all of these are concepts
that were present and vital in the social settings of the theologians
who then used them to try to understand how Jesus saves.[9] This is
not a criticism of their views; this is just how it works. As human
beings we understand new things by trying to find already-exist-
ing patterns in our world into which we can incorporate the new
experience or reality. Mystery, which is always new, is approached
intellectually through symbols and metaphors that we have already
available in our lives. Without these, mystery would be meaningless,
for we could never approach it at all or begin to incorporate it into
our worldviews. At the same time, this means that our efforts at
describing mystery will always be shaped by the circumstances of
our own existence. We will always, necessarily, write something of
ourselves into our descriptions of mystery, into our accounts of how
Jesus saves. While this allows us to draw nearer to the truth of salvation, it also means that we never have the pure, objective, untainted

account of how it functions. Instead, our theories and descriptions are provisional attempts at knowing something beyond our ken.

Second, the history of Christology (like the history of every other doctrine) is a long conversation among faithful communities and theologians who disagree with each other. Anselm wanted to correct Origen; Abelard wanted to correct Anselm. No theologian gets it exactly right, but there is truth and faith in the ongoing attempt of the larger Christian community to know the God we revere. One of my main teaching goals in any setting is to invite my students into the ongoing conversation of theology. So I assured my students that theology is just a conversation. Everyone can join in.

Beyond the Bible Study

One of the most compelling voices to enter the conversation about how Jesus saves in recent years is that of Delores Williams. In 1993 Williams wrote and Orbis Books published a book called *Sisters in the Wilderness: The Challenge of Womanist God-Talk*, a must-read for anyone interested in diving into contemporary Christology. While this rich text accomplishes a number of tasks, the most provocative is to launch a significant critique of all Christologies that place surrogacy at the heart of how Jesus saves.

Beginning with a critical reading of the story of Abraham, Sarah, and Hagar, Williams analyzes the history of surrogacy among African American women. During slavery, black women were forced into literal surrogacy, forced to bear children for white slaveholders and to raise the children of whites. While such coercive and literal surrogacy ended with slavery, Williams argues that factors such as poverty continue to pressure black women into voluntarily choosing social-role surrogacy, in which they fulfill the social role of another. Economic realities and social pressures lead many black women into employment where they care for the children of white couples, clean and cook for white families, and so on. Williams concludes that "surrogacy has been a negative force in African-American women's lives. It has been used by both men and women of the ruling class, as well as by some black men, to keep black women in the service of other people's needs and goals."[10]

This analysis of surrogacy leads Williams to question Christologies in which Jesus functions as a surrogate, in which "he stands in the place of someone else."[11] She is wary of any understanding of redemption that relies on a logic of surrogacy or substitution, where Jesus takes the debt, burden, or punishment of or responsibility for human sin upon himself. Such theories, Williams claims, give surrogacy "an aura of the sacred" and make it harder for black women to resist the negative effects of surrogacy in their lives. If we believe that God operates through surrogacy, how can we wholeheartedly reject it?

Williams asserts that theologies with a logic of surrogacy undergird human practices of social-role surrogacy that exploit black women. Yet note that Williams's argument is more far-reaching than the situation of African American women. In our contemporary world, some people suffer for the benefit of others, and this is seen as okay. When I buy clothing for my children, I can purchase well-made goods for a small fraction of my salary. The tags say they are made in Guatemala, China, or Mexico. I know, as do most consumers, that the living conditions of the workers who manufactured these clothes are not nearly as good as those of my family. It is because these workers are paid little that I can afford to buy nice things for my own children. By my own complacency, I tacitly accept not only the inequality, but also the system wherein my family benefits from the suffering of other families. That some suffer for the benefit of others—this is the heart of the logic of surrogacy that Williams critiques.

Also note that Williams is not claiming a direct causal link between surrogacy theologies and oppression. She does not state that *because* Christians often think of Jesus as standing in the place of sinful humanity, whites exploit black women and black women accept surrogacy roles. Instead, she simply acknowledges that how we think about God influences how we treat each other. This is an extremely straightforward claim, which few theologians would completely refute. It resonates with the observation of anthropologist Clifford Geertz (1926–2006), who characterizes religious and theological claims as both *models of* a community's understanding of God and *models for* human behavior.[12] The two cannot be fully separated, no matter how carefully we delineate between human and divine. How we understand God shapes our human behavior, and our human behavior shapes how we understand God. If we believe that God is kind and loving, then kindness and love will be our highest values. Likewise, if kindness and love are our highest values, as we attempt to understand who God is, we will speak of God as kind and loving. Williams's claim that how we envision God influences our human community is the flip side of the observation made above regarding theology, that our cultural and social location influences how we envision God. Just as our cultural patterns influence how we see God, how we see God influences our cultural patterns. Geertz's phrase "model of God and model for human behavior" succinctly captures the relationship of the two. This is a further example of the interconnections of systematic theology. What we say about how Jesus saves is connected to what we accept and reject in our daily lives.

Because of her appreciation for the interaction between visions of God and human behavior, Williams is highly critical of any theology that hinges on surrogacy, and particularly surrogate suffering. Patterns of behavior that are divinely endorsed (even if only for Jesus!) cannot be seen as entirely reprehensible. For this reason,

Williams locates salvation in the life and ministry of Jesus and rejects any notion that the cross is redemptive. Jesus' death on the cross, according to Williams, does not accomplish salvation but shows fully human sin, desecration, and defilement.[13] She writes:

> Humankind is, then, redeemed through Jesus' ministerial vision of life and not through his death. There is nothing divine in the blood of the cross. God does not intend black women's surrogacy experience. Neither can Christian faith affirm such an idea. Jesus did not come to be a surrogate. Jesus came for life, to show humans a perfect vision of ministerial relation that humans had very little knowledge of. As Christians, black women cannot forget the cross, but neither can they glorify it. To do so is to glorify suffering and to render their exploitation sacred. To do so is to glorify the sin of defilement.[14]

Williams gives a beautifully concise summary of several theories of atonement, descriptions of how Jesus saves that have been embraced by Christians in different times and places. Noting that we always use the tools at hand in our own culture to try to understand how Jesus saves, Williams takes this diversity of views as a liberating history that allows Christians to "use the language and sociopolitical thought of the time to render Christian ideas and principles understandable."[15] Thus, in eschewing salvation on the cross, Williams is participating in the same venerable tradition as Anselm and Abelard, offering a corrective to those theologians who have come before and doing so from a particular social location, in her case that of an African American woman. Her work is coherent, logical, thoughtful, and persuasive. Responsible theologians working on Christology after 1993 have to take Williams's argument into account.

While the first part of Williams's argument—that Christologies in which Jesus suffers as a surrogate undergird oppression— is extremely persuasive, her conclusion is difficult to accept. Many students, reading Williams for the first time, react with an almost violent rejection. Clearly, they claim, she does not understand the once-and-for-all nature of Jesus' sacrifice, the Christian injunction to suffer for others rather than allow others to suffer for us, the metaphysical size gap between God and humanity that necessitates different models of behavior, and so forth. The problem, they assert, is not with the view of salvation that follows a logic of surrogacy, but that this view is misunderstood. If we could explain surrogate salvation more clearly, if it were incorporated into Christian life in a more nuanced manner, things would get better. Yet if we take Geertz seriously, believing that models of God function as models for human behavior, these rebuttals fail. Envisioning God as saving through surrogate suffering will always, no matter how deftly described, undergird surrogate suffering among humanity.

Even among those who accept this analysis, many Christians find too much salvific power in the cross to accept Williams's conclusions completely. While oppression and surrogacy have been prominent in the experiences of African American women, and therefore must be taken into account in Christian theology, it is also true that many African American women experience the cross of Christ as liberating. In the same year that Williams published *Sisters in the Wilderness*, theologian M. Shawn Copeland published an essay titled "'Wading through Many Sorrows': Toward a Theology of Suffering in Womanist Perspective." Here Copeland, like Williams, recounts the ways in which Christianity was used to oppress enslaved African and African American women and asserts that this should be taken into account in current theology. Copeland writes:

> In its teaching, theologizing, preaching, and practice, this Christianity sought to bind the slaves to their condition by inculcating caricatures of the cardinal virtues of patience, long-suffering, forbearance, love, faith, and hope. Thus, to distance itself from any form of masochism, even Christian

masochism, a theology of suffering from womanist perspective must reevaluate those virtues in light of Black women's experiences.[16]

Unlike Williams, however, Copeland focuses on the ways in which enslaved Africans resisted this oppressive force, highlighting the positive meaning that was seen in the cross. She argues that those who sang of the cross in spirituals did so

> not because they were masochistic and enjoyed suffering. Rather, the enslaved Africans sang because they saw on the rugged wooden planks One who had endured what was their daily portion. The cross was treasured because it enthroned the One who went all the way with them and for them. The enslaved Africans sang because they saw the result of the cross—triumph over the principalities and powers of death, triumph over evil in this world.[17]

Enslaved Africans and African Americans continue to find meaning and resources for resistance within the same Christian stories that were used as weapons against them. For this reason Copeland declares that "Black women under chattel slavery freed the cross of Christ. Their steadfast commitment honored that cross and the One who died for all and redeemed it from Christianity's vulgar misuse."[18]

Following insights such as Copeland's, JoAnne Terrell argues passionately for the importance of the cross for African American women in a book titled *Power in the Blood? The Cross in the African American Experience*.[19] The question then becomes, for Terrell and for many others, how to learn from Williams's brilliant critique while holding on to the redemptive power of the cross, how to reconceptualize Christology such that the cross is salvific but the logic behind salvation does not undergird exploitation. This is one of the most pressing issues in current Christology.

Scrunchies and Systematics Revisited

Earlier in this chapter I used the metaphor of weaving scrunchies for the task of systematic theology, and went so far as to describe some characteristics of good theology in scrunchie-inspired terms. I said that theology should be flexible enough to gather in yet strong enough to hold; it should be individual and communal; it should be functional and beautiful; it should be a possession that offers comfort and connection. I hope that in the course of this chapter some slightly more concrete considerations for good theology, and good scrunchies, have emerged. First, Christian theology, like that first scrunchie in the Guatemalan orphanage, is a hand-me-down. It is a tradition, which literally means that it is handed down from one to the other.[20] The best Christian theology takes the tradition seriously. This does not mean that what has been handed down cannot be argued with, altered, challenged, revised, or refuted. A brilliant theologian may choose to reject the claims of Nicea and Chalcedon. But she will not do so lightly or without good reason. Second, theology, again like those Guatemalan scrunchies, is made up of the materials at hand. We weave with the resources of our particular communities, cultures, and locations. Remembering this inspires humility about our own theological pronouncements, as well as reverence for the flexible strength of the good news. Third, theology, like scrunchies, needs to work well in the real world. If it is beautiful and logically coherent but hurts someone, we need to reweave. If we believe that Jesus loves those on the margins of society but our theology reinforces marginalization, we need to rethink.

Jesus Still Saves

The two-word declaration "Jesus saves," written on a highway overpass in the Appalachian Mountains, fails to capture the complexity of Christology. It cannot contain the mystery of the Logos, the second person of the Trinity, revelation of the one God who is three. Nor can it convey the mystery of two natures in one person, of Jesus Christ, fully human and fully divine. Likewise, it masks the rich history of Christian communities struggling to understand how Jesus saves, to articulate this good news in terms and concepts that make it real in everyday life. The statement "Jesus saves" obscures the disagreements and developments in two thousand years of theological conversation on this topic.

Learning about the mystery and the history of Christology can be wildly disconcerting. The comfort of imagining that the phrase "Jesus saves" points to one simple reality that everyone in the community knows and trusts evaporates, and we are left with many questions, multiple explanations, changing visions, and fluid understandings. Learning about this can also be deeply liberating. It acknowledges real differences within Christian perspectives that we have experienced, even if they have gone unnamed. It recognizes the incredible strength of a truth so profound it makes sense in multiple ways, to diverse groups, in varied settings. And it invites us to join in the long tradition of inspiration and discernment, conversation and contention, that is Christian systematic theology. Learning more about the complexity of Christology takes away the simplicity of "Jesus saves," but it offers us the opportunity to explore more deeply the salvation given in Jesus Christ.

Location, Location, Location
Shawnthea Monroe

Some Christian traditions and denominations sit quite comfortably with creeds. They recite the Apostles' Creed every Sunday in worship, or they intone the Nicene Creed at the Eucharist, or they consult the Westminster Confession in making churchly decisions. I, however, am a pastor in the United Church of Christ, a denomination that, along with some others, has an innate suspicion of creeds. As inheritors of the congregational tradition, which tends to raise an eyebrow anytime religious freedom is restricted, we in the UCC place the emphasis not on creeds but on how the Spirit shapes each Christian's faith. We lean hard on the view that human language is limited, unable to express the full experience of any person's relationship with God.

The upside of being noncreedal is that our churches are remarkably diverse when it comes to theology. In my former congregation, Seventh-day Adventists happily shared hymnals with Unitarians. But there is also a downside to being noncreedal. Creeds are good teachers of theology, and many people in the United Church of Christ cannot talk about theology because they have not learned the language or the traditional categories through creeds. Pastors often make this problem worse. Given the breadth of the theological viewpoints in our churches, we preachers are tempted to shy away from making specific faith statements for fear that someone might take offense or feel slighted. In an attempt to avoid taking sides, we say nothing specific or risky. We are far braver when it comes to social issues like poverty or racism, where there is a clear right and wrong.

Yet over the years, I've discovered that the best way to minister in the midst of theological diversity is not to be vague but to be clear and specific about theology. Part of my job is to help others make theological sense of their lives, so whether I'm talking to people in the pulpit or the classroom or the grocery store, my aim is to articulate a specific theological point of view. I think of it as hanging a plumb line, a steady marker on the landscape of Christian faith. My intent is not to indoctrinate but to provide a reference point. If people understand where I am in my faith, it helps them locate themselves on the theological map and possibly navigate into new territory.

Shannon explores the doctrine of Christology in two ways. First by way of a timeline of the life of Jesus Christ, then through a sampling of historical models. I find her first approach most intriguing for it presses Christians to locate where salvation occurs within the narrative of the Jesus event. For our purposes I think it is helpful to drop two plumb lines on the life of Christ, identifying distinct points that represent two common understandings of Jesus Christ present in the church today. In fact, these two positions are the Christologies I run into most frequently among the members of my own congregation. What a Christian believes about Jesus Christ does not stand in isolation, but affects every other aspect of faith. Therefore, I want to trace how each of these two Christological positions might shape, inform, and limit the Christian life through everything from hymns to holidays, social action to sacraments. I will look at what is at stake in these two positions, what is gained as well as what is lost as a sort of theological cost-benefit analysis. My point is not to advocate for a particular position, but to model a way of "doing theology" in the midst of everyday church life so that the message is coherent.

On the one hand, there are the *Resurrection Christians*, people who believe that the key to understanding what Jesus has done is found in the events of Easter morning. The empty tomb is an astonishing demonstration that God has the power to save; in the resurrection, God's full intentions toward humanity are revealed. Furthermore, Resurrection Christians, in the way I will use the term, generally believe in the bodily resurrection of Christ rather than in a spiritual resurrection.

On the other hand, there are *Life and Ministry Christians*, people who believe that Jesus' power to save was revealed in his ministry and healing. By giving us a model for human life that was completely God-centered and selfless, Jesus offered a way of living that ran counter to the prevailing culture, both then and now, and has the power to transform individual lives and ultimately the world.

Resurrection Christians believe that in Jesus' death on the cross, God was at work reconciling the world, doing something that we human beings could not do on our own—saving humanity. Life and Ministry Christians, on the other hand, tend to view the cross as the inevitable result of Jesus' radical life of obedient faith rather than as a necessary part of salvation. In sum, Life and Ministry Christians see Jesus as a role model, as one who transforms our lives by setting before us the pattern of his own faithful life and calling us to follow him on that path. Resurrection Christians see Jesus as a savior, as one who acted on our behalf to liberate us from captivity and now calls us to respond with gratitude, joy, and obedience to the grace we have been given.

Before I explore these specific Christological "plumb lines" and see how each one can shape and give rise to different Christian practices, I want to note that dividing Christians neatly into these two positions is misleading. Real theological positions are rarely so clean and clearly defined. People who place primary emphasis on the resurrection are usually deeply invested and interested in the life and ministry of Jesus, just as people whose primary understanding of Christ is rooted in his life and ministry may also hold the resurrection as the ultimate vindication of that work.[21] The point is that almost everyone has a particular Christological lens through which she or he views the rest of the Christian story, a lens that brings different things into focus. So to promote discussion and to show what is at stake in Christology, I'm going to sacrifice nuance for clarity's sake. Let's begin with a Sunday morning visit to two hypothetical congregations, one full of Resurrection Christians and the other full of Life and Ministry Christians, just to discover what difference Christology can make in congregational life.

Our Savior's Church

Our Savior's Church is all about the resurrection. The stained-glass windows depict the women at the tomb on one side and the risen Christ, wounded hands extended, on the other. The central symbol is an empty cross, which hangs above the chancel. The theological furniture of the communion table, the baptismal font, and the pulpit form a perfect V in the worship space. On the communion table sits a Bible with two tall candles on either side. Built in an era when every architectural line and flourish had theological meaning, Our Savior's sanctuary is oriented so that the congregation worships facing east, toward the rising Son.

Even if you couldn't see the building, you could still make out Our Savior's Christology by the sound of the congregation's worship. The service begins with the hymn "Sing Praise to God Who Reigns Above," ending with the line "Cast each false idol from the throne, for Christ is Lord, and Christ alone: to God all praise and glory." Later in the service we sing "At the Name of Jesus," that beautiful song based on Philippians 2:6-11:

> Humbled for a season, to receive a Name
> From the lips of sinners, unto whom he came.
> Faithfully he bore it, spotless to the last,
> Brought it back victorious, when from death he passed.[22]

The Scripture text for the day comes from the letters of Paul, where Resurrection Christians find their scriptural center. Bodily resurrection is the engine that drives Paul's Christology, and the apostle has hard words for anyone who denies it. His resurrection argument is beautifully developed in this morning's passage from 1 Corinthians 15:

> Now if Christ is proclaimed as raised from the dead, how can some of you say there is no resurrection of the dead? If there is no resurrection of the dead, then Christ has not been raised; and if Christ has not been raised, then our proclamation has been in vain and your faith has been in vain. We are even found to be misrepresenting God, because we testified of God that he raised Christ—whom he did not raise if it is true that the dead are not raised. For if the dead are not raised, then Christ has not been raised. If Christ has not been raised, your faith is futile and you are still in your sins. Then those also who have died in Christ have perished. (15:12-18)

If Life and Ministry Christians emphasize our life in the present and how it can be patterned after the way Jesus lived his life, the Resurrection Christians hear Paul, at the conclusion of this passage, raising a question about whether life in the present is really enough: "If for this life only we have hoped in Christ, we are of all people most to be pitied" (15:19). Paul believes there is no salvation apart from the resurrection. For Resurrection Christians, this is a word that informs and inspires.

The sermon is firmly rooted in the biblical text, because the Resurrection Christians at Our Savior's have built their faith on what God has done in Jesus Christ. They want to hear the "old, old story," the witness of Scripture, and they might be disappointed if the sermon strays too far from the text. The preacher ties in current events to the extent that they shed light on God's reconciling work through Jesus Christ. The sermon ends with a word about how the good news found in 1 Corinthians strengthens our faith and gives us hope in a weary world, though there is no specific call to action or suggestion of what particular form that hope might take. After the sermon we sing a hymn of interior piety and prepare for a time of prayer and reflection.

As we leave the church, we find a large plaque with the names of all the church members who have died in service to their country, with the words "No Greater Love Hath Any Man" inscribed in bronze. Walking toward the fellowship hall, we see a side garden with a columbarium, the final resting place for the ashes of members. Even Our Savior's Web site reflects a Resurrection Christology. Log on to the home page and click the "What We Believe" button and you will find a creedal statement that begins with the words "We believe in the one triune God and in God's only Son, Jesus Christ."

First Church

First Church is a Life and Ministry congregation. As you drive up to First Church, the first thing you notice is the "Peace Now" banner that hangs over the front door. There is no stained glass, only clear windows providing an unobstructed view of the world outside. If we visit during Advent or Lent, we will see a cross hanging in the sanctuary, but not at this time of year.

The communion table is decorated with a half dozen prayer shawls knitted by the women's fellowship, with the Bible off to the side. The pulpit, decorated with a parament woven from recycled materials, stands to the left of the communion table, but there is no baptismal font. The font is brought out only on Sundays when a baptism is to take place during the service. In the pew racks we find hymnals as well as envelopes for a special disaster offering.

There is also literature on the "Green Church" initiative and an order form for "Fair Trade Coffee."

The opening hymn is "Out of Need and Out of Custom," which concludes with the comforting words "God of human transformation, for your presence now we pray; lead us ever on the journey as we gather here today." At the close of worship, we join together in singing "Sister, Let Me Be Your Servant." Sometimes the elders at First Church request more traditional hymns, such as "In the Garden" or "We Would Be Building." But even when the music comes from a different era, the Life and Ministry point of view comes through: Jesus is our Savior because he is our guide and model.

The text for this Sunday is from Luke. If Life and Ministry Christians had to put their chips down on one piece of Scripture, it would probably be the Great Commandment (Matt. 22:34-40; Mark 12:28-31; Luke 10:25-28). We listen as the lawyer in Luke's account stands in for all of us and asks:

> "Teacher, . . . what must I do to inherit eternal life?" He said to him, "What is written in the law? What do you read there?" He answered, "You shall love the Lord your God with all your heart, and with all your soul, and with all your strength, and with all your mind; and your neighbor as yourself." And he said to him, "You have given the right answer; do this, and you will live." (10:25-28)

(Of course, the lawyer wants a more precise legal definition of "neighbor," which leads into the parable of the good Samaritan, another important part of the Life and Ministry canon.) Taken at his word in this passage, Jesus locates salvation in the daily acts of loving God and loving neighbor. Eternal life begins here and now. Viewed through this lens, the work of Jesus Christ is all about the small decisions, the "What Would Jesus Do?" moments.

In a Life and Ministry church like First Church, the sermon is an opportunity to bring the critical issues of social justice into focus through the use of Scripture and to help the congregation determine what course of action they will take. This morning the preacher begins the sermon by recasting the roles in the parable, giving Luke's story a modern twist. The man is a naturalized American citizen, originally from Saudi Arabia, when he is arrested by the National Security Agency after 9/11. He is imprisoned at Guantánamo Bay without benefit of legal counsel, where he is tortured and abandoned, forgotten by the side of the road. Two people pass by, a Democrat and a Republican, but neither politician makes a move to help the man. The Samaritan turns out to be a Christian, someone from First Church. But the conclusion of the story is left for us to finish. The preacher asks, "Will we stop and help, even though the man isn't one of us? Even though he may be our sworn enemy? What will we do? What would Jesus do?" We know what Jesus would do, and we are given clear direction about what we should do next.

After the sermon there is a moment for mission, during which a representative for the local homeless shelter talks about the need for more volunteers. Everyone is encouraged to sign up, and she ends by paraphrasing the words of Jesus in Matthew 25:40: "As you have done to the least of these, so have you done to me."

Leaving First Church, we see a sign that says, "The Worship Is Over, Let the Service Begin." In the narthex there is a row of sign-up sheets and posters for special events and service projects. There is also a grocery cart where you can drop off donations for the emergency food pantry. And if you check First's Web site for a statement of faith, it begins, "We are called to lives of faithful service as followers of Jesus Christ." First Church locates the saving work of Jesus Christ in his Life and Ministry.

Though Our Savior's and First Church are fictional congregations, each is an amalgam of churches I have visited, and every detail is taken from real life. What I'm trying to draw out is the variety of ways two distinct Christologies can shape a service of worship and, in turn, shape a congregation. We even carry our particular Christologies with us when we worship in other settings.

There are other ways one's Christological point of view is expressed in worship. For example, consider the different roles of Scripture in the two services. At Our Savior's, Scripture is the focus of the sermon, while at First Church, Scripture is just the starting point. What we believe about Jesus Christ affects *how* we read Scripture, what we *do* with Scripture, even what parts of the Bible we read. This is especially true because the New Testament does not give just one clear witness about Jesus Christ. Multiple narratives are operating, especially in the four Gospels. As a result, we tend to create a personal canon, a collection of those parts of the Bible that resonate with our personal theological view. There is no sin in this scriptural self-selection. Even Martin Luther believed that not all parts of the Bible are equal. His standard was that whatever "presses Christ" takes precedence over less Christocentric passages. The version of Christ you are pressing helps determine what passages take precedence.

Another way Christology is expressed in a service is by what comes after the sermon in the order of worship. In the standard *ordo,* or order of worship, we begin with a call to worship, and recognizing that God is present, we confess our sins and usually sing a hymn of praise. Following that comes the proclamation of the Word through the reading of Scripture and the preaching of a sermon. Next comes the response of the people. At Our Savior's, the response takes the form of a hymn of reflection followed by prayers. This focus on interior piety as the originating place of human response fits with a Resurrection Christology: God has done something for us, and our response is first to meditate on what that means. At First Church, however, the response takes the form of a moment for mission. The focus is on putting faith in action by following the model of Jesus Christ, the moral exemplar. Again, this response coheres with a Life and Ministry Christology: God has given us a model for life in Jesus Christ, and now we need to get busy living it out. This is not to say that the difference between these two Christologies is about inner piety versus missional action. Every Christology contains elements of piety and mission, but each Christology places the emphasis in different locations.

Christology and the Liturgical Year

If we step back from the particularities of a Sunday worship experience, we begin to see how different Christologies can shape the entire liturgical year. For example, the favored Sunday for Resurrection Christians is Easter, whereas Life and Ministry Christians prefer the empowerment of Pentecost. Yet there is more to this liturgical shaping than picking a favorite holiday. If we develop a coherent theological understanding of the salvific work of Jesus Christ, it becomes part of how we experience and celebrate the entire Christian year.

For Resurrection Christians, Easter is the singular event around which the rest of the calendar is arranged. But it is not like a roller coaster, with one high peak and a sudden descent. The resurrection is more like a tuning fork we strike and set on each part of the liturgical year, listening for the distinctive hum of God's transformative power. Knowing that Christ is risen casts all other moments in a certain light. (It is like the ending of Mark's Gospel, when the disciples are told to return to Galilee where the story began, but this time with the understanding that the human Jesus is also the risen Christ.) At Christmas we might notice how the surprise of the incarnation is a precursor to the surprise of the resurrection—each event defying human understanding of the way the world works. The fire and wind of Pentecost can be interpreted as fulfillment of the promises made by the risen Christ. Even in everyday moments of ordinary time, we look for the many moods and expressions of Easter. This kind of theological coherence creates an interpretive instinct, which in turn allows people to better understand their lives in relationship to God.

The same is true for Life and Ministry Christians, but the sound of the tuning fork is slightly different. For Life and Ministry Christians, there is no *kairos*, one meaning-filled moment when everything comes together. Instead, we hallow *chronos*, the ordinary time. Each season of the liturgical year brings a new phase and nuance to our understanding of the person of Jesus Christ. In Christmas we find the gifts of humility and dependence. In Lent he is the model of obedience and selfless love. Even in his betrayal and arrest, Jesus continues to heal, comfort, and instruct. Throughout the year Jesus lives in his moment, modeling a Spirit-filled life in faithful obedience to God. We still celebrate all the peaks and valleys of the Christian year, but the coherent message we create is about how to embody Christlike lives here and now.

Sacramental Christology

No place does our particular Christology find expression more clearly than in the celebration of the sacraments.[23] This makes sense. We believe that God's grace is especially present in Baptism and Communion; therefore, how we define and understand that grace shapes what we believe is happening in the sacrament, which in turn determines the words we use to describe it.

Baptism. In the United Church of Christ's *Book of Worship*, the officiating minister is given a number of choices in terms of baptismal liturgy, but most of the options lean toward a Life and Ministry view of the resurrection. Here is a sample of the words of address:

The sacrament of baptism is an outward and visible sign of the grace of God. Inasmuch as the promise of the gospel is not only to us but also to our children, baptism with water and the Holy Spirit is the mark of their acceptance into the care of Christ's church, the sign and seal of their participation in God's forgiveness, and the beginning of their growth into full Christian faith and discipleship.[24]

The address gives an order to what is happening. First, the child is being adopted into the life of the church, and in most UCC baptismal services, the congregation vows to help raise the child in the Christian faith. The second meaning of baptism is as a sign and seal of the child's *participation* in God's forgiveness. It is not something that has happened, but a new opportunity to be part of God's reconciling work in the world.

Finally, the child is baptized so he or she might grow in faith and discipleship—that is, the believing is part and parcel of the doing. Clearly, what is offered in baptism is an opportunity to enter into the family of Christ and begin to live a Christlike life. There is no identification of the child as a sinner, no language about death and new life, no reference to the resurrection.

The same Christology is expressed in one of our favorite baptismal hymns, "In Water We Grow." The end of the second verse beautifully sums up the liturgy: "In Christ recreated by love's cleansing art, self-will and self-hatred dissolve and depart." This baptismal service is shaped by a Life and Ministry Christology.

Compare this liturgy with the traditional baptismal prayer from the 1978 *Lutheran Book of Worship*, which reads in part:

In the waters of Jordan your Son was baptized by John and anointed with the Spirit. By the baptism of his own death and resurrection your beloved Son has set us free from the bondage to sin and death, and has opened the way to the joy and freedom of everlasting life. He made water a sign of the kingdom and of cleansing and rebirth. In obedience to his command, we make disciples of all nations, baptizing them in the name of the Father, and of the Son, and of the Holy Spirit.[25]

Unlike the UCC liturgy, which expresses a Life and Ministry Christology, this prayer outlines a Resurrection Christological point of view. Jesus was baptized by John with water and the Spirit, but our baptism is accomplished through Christ's death and resurrection. It is this implied baptism of blood that brings about the gift of grace—freedom from bondage and sin, and access to eternal life. There is no trace of adoption language; there is no suggestion that this is the beginning of a process of growth into full Christian faith and fellowship. What occurs in baptism is the work of God in Jesus Christ, and it is accomplished once and for all. Our further participation is not part of that work, only a response to it. I am reminded of another baptismal hymn, "We Know That Christ Is Raised," in which the second verse begins, "We share by water in his [Christ's] saving death." This is Resurrection Christology.

Of course, these are two stark examples chosen because they reveal the ways in which what we say when we baptize communicates precisely what we believe about Jesus Christ. Most ministers have a wide range of choices when it comes to crafting baptismal liturgy, and there isn't one correct way to do things. What is important is that we intentionally examine our sacramental language to make sure it is a faithful expression of a coherent Christology.

Communion. There are five images of or ways of understanding the Eucharist in the New Testament. First, it is an act of participating in creation, in which the creatures and part of the natural world are brought together by the creator God. Second, there is a reenactment understanding, in which we gather for the Lord's

Supper to "drink and remember." The third interpretation is that of communion—the whole family of God gathered at the table, eating together in one spirit. There is also a "Eucharistic" understanding, in which we give thanks to God for the gift of Jesus Christ. And finally, there is the eschatological interpretation, in which the meal is a foretaste of the heavenly banquet to come. All of these interpretations are present when we celebrate the sacrament of Communion, but the emphasis changes depending on the community's understanding of Jesus Christ.

If we come to the table with a Resurrection Christology, then we place greater emphasis on the Eucharistic language and the eschatological promise. The sacrament is first and foremost a statement of who Christ is and the hope we have: "Christ has died. Christ has risen. Christ will come again."

On the other hand, a Life and Ministry Christology would emphasize the communion/community aspect of the sacrament. The United Church of Christ *Book of Worship* offers these words in the communion prayer: "We ask you to send your Holy Spirit on this bread and wine, on our gifts, and on us. Strengthen your universal church that it may be the champion of peace and justice in the world."[26] This meal is not primarily about a future promise; this meal has implications for what we do when we leave the table. What happens when Jesus returns is less critical than what happens today.

I don't want to suggest that one coherent Christology can always be teased out through observing the sacramental practices of a church. In fact, I think many people—even pastors—are blind to the theological implications of what we do or say on a Sunday. Yet, while I do not advocate for a particular Christology, I believe we need to carefully attend to what we say and do, especially around the sacraments, to avoid theological accidents.

Christology and Tragedy

Up to this point, we have been exploring the ways in which different Christologies might influence and shape the everyday practices of a Christian community. The ideal is to create practices that are coherent with the underlying theology so that what we do and what we believe inform and support each other. This is particularly important when something awful and out of the ordinary occurs. When tragedy strikes, a community needs the resources of a strong theological narrative, for such a narrative helps us make sense of events and moves us to act, even when we are too stunned to think clearly. Perhaps especially in times of tragedy, our actions are deeply influenced by what we believe about Jesus.

I am writing during one of the worst flood seasons in American history. The levees along the Mississippi and the Missouri rivers are giving way, flooding towns and putting crops underwater. The call has gone out for sandbags, cleaning kits, generators, and food donations. Toll-free numbers are available to aid volunteers in finding out where help is most needed in the Midwest. Many churches are taking special collections to help our friends and neighbors whose lives have been affected by the heavy storms.

When disasters like this strike, you can count on Life and Ministry Christians to respond. There is no question what Jesus would do: Christ has no hands but yours—and he needs you to fill sandbags. For people who believe Jesus' power was centered in his activity, there is no doubt about what happens next. When there is a need for action, Life and Ministry Christians are efficient and effective. God's redeeming love in Jesus Christ determines the response, and help is on the way.

Resurrection Christians lack this pressing imperative to act. Their first impulse might be to pray, not to pay. This is not to say that Resurrection Christians won't offer assistance, just that their understanding of the Christian faith doesn't require them to respond.

But what do we do when a tragedy moves beyond our ability to help? Last month the bodies of two young girls were found in a ditch along a road in rural Oklahoma. The two had been shot multiple times at close range, and authorities are at a loss as to motive or even the number of perpetrators involved. The local news station interviewed the grandfather of one of the girls, who said, "It's hurting us very much. No one can understand how something like this happens." There isn't anything I can do to help this man or his grieving family. No special collection will heal this loss; no volunteers are needed to put the house back in order. When a tragedy like this happens, the only possible response is theological.

Resurrection Christians have such a response. They believe that God's redeeming work in Jesus Christ is an ongoing project to be consummated outside of history, not necessarily within it. Even the tragic death of a child is not beyond the power of God's redemption, but it is a redemption in which we must trust. There is nothing to be done, only a hope to be proclaimed, even through tears. While this theological response may seem like cold comfort, it is the only way we can endure losses of this magnitude.

Christology at Its Best

So far, we have explored two particular Christologies, how they shape and influence Christian practices, and how they equip Christians to respond to natural disasters and senseless tragedy. Each particular view of the salvific work of Jesus has natural advantages and disadvantages when it comes to daily life. Furthermore, every Christology reaches its zenith in a different moment in human experience.

People who lay claim to a Life and Ministry understanding of Jesus are great social reformers, for it is a Christology that is most useful when it comes to social action. Jesus himself sets the agenda in Luke 4:18-19:

> "The Spirit of the Lord is upon me,
>> because he has anointed me to bring good news to the
>>> poor.
> He has sent me to proclaim release to the captives
>> and recovery of sight to the blind,
>>> to let the oppressed go free,
> to proclaim the year of the Lord's favor."

Called as participants in God's ongoing work of reconciliation, Life and Ministry Christians are blessed with a sense that they can make a difference—and are called by God to do so. Energy and resilience flow from this understanding of the work of Jesus Christ. It also comes with a certain sense of built-in success, for even small efforts make a difference. Again, we recall Matthew 25:40: "As you have done to the least of these, so have you done to me" (my paraphrase). For Life and Ministry Christians, there is no faith apart from action.

Yet if we view social action from a Resurrection perspective, the picture is far gloomier. Resurrection Christians place a lot of emphasis on the agency of God, for it is God who has accomplished our salvation through the resurrection of Jesus. There is also a keen sense that nothing will be completed in this life; everything, even social action, is a work in progress. Recall what Jesus says to the disciples in Matthew 26:11: "For you always have the poor with you, but you will not always have me." Yes, we're called to lives of obedient service in response to God's gift of salvation through Christ, but let's not have any illusions that we will actually solve any of these problems. If the kingdom is going to come, it won't be by our efforts. When it comes to social action, a Resurrection Christology is not the engine that pulls the train. Instead, the moment when Resurrection Christians reach their strength is at the time of death.

I knew a lay minister who was an avid reader of popular theology. Over time he had become persuaded by the argument that Jesus' resurrection was not an actual event, but rather a spiritual experience shared by the disciples that enabled them to carry on Jesus' work in the world, seeking peace and justice for all people. In other words, he had become a specific kind of Life and Ministry Christian. But there was a problem: he found himself unable to officiate at funerals. Through his Christological lens, any suggestion of a bodily resurrection was unsupported by the facts. The only word he had to offer grieving families was one of remembrance: the deceased had lived a good life in the pattern of Christ and should inspire us to do the same. The folks in his small rural parish felt this was not enough good news and told him so.

For those who believe in the bodily resurrection of Christ—and see it as the defining moment in the Christ event—funerals are a moment of truth. We approach the grave not as people without hope, but as people who believe that, through the resurrection, Jesus has conquered death. Yes, we still experience death, but it is not the last word on us, nor does it fill us with fear. The resurrection traces a trajectory for human life that arcs beyond the horizon of our own death. Not everything will work out in this life. There will be disappointments—personal as well as communal— and times of tragedy and sorrow for which there is no easy fix. Yet the God of Jesus Christ speaks a word of comfort, hope, and redemption through the empty tomb, a word that can transform our mourning into praise.

Last Word

Every Christian has a particular understanding of who Jesus Christ is and what it means that Jesus is our Savior. We might be Resurrection Christians or Life and Ministry Christians or something altogether different. What we believe, explicitly or implicitly, about Jesus Christ influences who we are, how we worship, how we act, even how we respond to tragedies. The key is to become Christologically self-aware. For if we understand our particular Christology, then we can craft ways of worshipping and living that are coherent with our beliefs. Out of this coherence comes a resilient faith, capable of supporting us come what may.

Three

Sin

The Work That Sin Can Do
Shannon Craigo-Snell

Sin has gone out of fashion. Well, *sinning* has timeless appeal, but the discourse and concepts of sin have gone out of style. Today the idea that all of humanity is deeply tainted by sin, such that our choices are often irrational and our moral compass constantly askew, is not part of our public discourse. The discourse of sin has been watered down almost beyond recognition. "Sinful" is an appetizing adjective on the dessert menu, and virtue is spending an hour at the gym. To understand this change, it is helpful to remember the brief discussion of modernity in chapter 1. In the modern period, people in the West started to think of the human person primarily as a rational, free, autonomous individual. We began to have near-infinite hope in the prospects of human progress and incredible optimism about what the human person could accomplish. This view of the human person did not fit well with older theological understandings of the human person as fundamentally marred by sin nor with the notion that humanity is collectively fallen. Sin, once understood as a serious distortion of the person that affects all of us, together, was replaced by more amenable concepts, such as error, bad choices, and poor individual morality.[1] In this chapter I argue that we lost some profound Christian wisdom in this transition. A sturdy Christian doctrine of sin offers us three things we desperately need: explanatory power, conviction, and relief. In this chapter, after a few preliminary historical remarks, I will outline three distinct, sturdy Christian views of sin that are part of the tradition and operative today.

Historical Background

The scriptural roots of the doctrine of sin also hearken back to chapter 1, to the stories of creation in Genesis. The account of Adam, Eve, the serpent, and the forbidden fruit forms the backdrop for Christian understandings of sin. This is not because contemporary Christian theologians are reading the story literally or imagining fruit as the ultimate downfall. Rather, embedded in this symbolic story are theological points crucial to mainstream Christianity. First, creation is good. Sin and evil come later. Sin is not a remnant of what was before God created. This point guards against possible understandings of sin and evil as intransigent characteristics of chaos or matter that linger after God shapes such chaos or matter into creation. It also forestalls dualistic readings that identify sin and evil with materiality and view good and evil as being on equal footing. God creates all of being, and it is good. Then sin and evil arrive on the scene. These do not have the same status as being, but rather are negations of being, privations of the good. Second, the arrival of sin and evil comes through humanity. Adam and Eve freely choose to eat the fruit, to disobey God, to prioritize their own desire and curiosity above their relationship with the Creator.

This is not to say (although some theologians do) that humans are the only causal forces involved. The conditions for the possibility of sin were there, somehow, in paradise. Robert Williams notes that the serpent was present as well, symbolizing the presence of some persuasive power, negligible in comparison to God but able to tempt humans.[2]

Another significant biblical source for reflecting on sin is the writings of Paul, particularly the letter to the Romans. While this text contains an enormous amount of insight into sin, I will highlight two moves Paul makes that have been particularly influential to the tradition. First, in a section extolling the free gift of grace in Jesus Christ, Paul writes that "sin came into the world through one man, and death came through sin, and so death spread to all because all have sinned" (Rom. 5:12). The main point here is the abundant and expansive grace of God, which in Jesus Christ reaches even further than the influence of sin. Many theologians have also inferred from this writing that Adam's sin marks the entry of sin into all of humanity, from which no one is exempt or excepted. Second, Paul also describes sin as a kind of slavery. Again, he speaks of sin in the context of grace, of being slaves to God. Yet he also offers a compelling depiction of an inner conflict within the self. He writes, "I do not understand my own actions. For I do not do what I want, but I do the very thing I hate" (Rom. 7:15). Here Paul portrays sin as a binding force to which humanity is enslaved, a force that is more than poor human choices that leave the human being neutral and untouched.

These are some of the biblical roots to the doctrine of original sin. In Christian traditions, original sin refers to the fallen condition of all of humanity. Every human being, by virtue of being part of humanity in which sin takes place, is fallen. Our understanding is darkened, our desires disordered, our will distorted. Theologians have described original sin in many different ways and argued whether it is transmitted by influence, inheritance, contagion, and so on. What these various descriptions share is the affirmation that original sin is a profoundly communal reality, the common lot of humanity.

The ideas in Paul's text come up again in the works of Augustine, whose theology has profoundly shaped the ongoing history of the doctrine of sin. As I did with Paul, here also I will shamefully limit my discussion to two points within an **abundance** of insights. After his conversion to Christianity, Augustine argued against Manichaeism, a school of thought to which he had once subscribed. This form of Gnosticism held a dualistic **view** in which the world is an arena of conflict between good and evil, light and darkness, spirituality and materiality. Followers of Manichaeism understood themselves to be divine spirits, or particles of light, entrapped in material bodies that were susceptible to physical suffering. This often led to practices of severe asceticism and denial of the body.[3] The converted Augustine refuted this view with a Christian doctrine of creation that affirms all being—including the material world—as good and from God. In this context, Augustine identifies sin and evil as a privation of the good, stemming from the disorderly choices of humans. Humans are created to be in loving relationship with God as the supreme good. When we honor and love God above all else, our various parts and passions are well ordered and function smoothly together. In contrast, when we choose to honor and love lesser goods, we get all out of whack. In Augustine's more elegant prose, "Evil is a turning away from immutable goods and a turning towards changeable goods."[4] This characterizes evil not as a bad will, or a bad object of desire, or a bad anything at all. Instead, it is the lack of a good, the loss of humanity's well-ordered love. Augustine's description of evil is a brilliant piece of theology that acknowledges the ubiquitous experience of evil and sin without granting evil any status in the created world. Rather, it is the voluntary, free choice of humans to love the lesser good. Evil is neither inherent in material reality nor a worthy adversary of the almighty God in some cosmic battle. It is merely the result of humanity's misuse of freedom.

Later in his career, Augustine argued against a group influenced by the monk Pelagius. We do not have any of Pelagius's writings, so his position is inferred from Augustine's arguments against him. With that caveat in mind, the Pelagian position appears to have been quite optimistic about humanity's ability to resist sin, obey the commands of God, and live a highly moral life. In particular, Pelagians believed that a human person can make the first move toward living a godly life. The reasoning ran something like this: God has commanded us to live ethically; therefore, we must be able to do so. Inherent in the Pelagian view was a sense of the human person as morally neutral and therefore able to choose well or badly. While Adam set a bad example for the rest of humanity, he did not introduce sin in some way that made it universally present or inescapable for the rest of humanity.[5]

Before describing Augustine's response to Pelagianism, I want to linger for a moment on how attractive this view is. Indeed, I think it is prevalent in many Christian communities across denominations, particularly in America. Pelagianism has a view of freedom that many of us find to be good common sense. Freedom is choosing between options. If we are responsible for making a bad choice, we must be able to make a good one. If we cannot choose the good, it does not make sense to hold us accountable for choosing the bad. Likewise, the Pelagian notion that we can take the first step toward right relation with God resonates deeply with a commonsense notion of Christianity as entailing rewards and punishments for our behavior. God tells us what to do and how to live. If we do what we are told, we go to heaven. If not, we go to hell. (Or, somewhat more subtly in contemporary prosperity gospel accounts, if we do what we are told, we live an abundant life now.

If not, we never realize our full potential.) God does God's part, including giving us ethical guidelines, and we do ours, including following them. In the land of the American dream, the notion that if we work hard and do the right thing, we can achieve success is deeply inscribed in our communal psyche—so deeply, in fact, that many faithful Christians think that the proverb "God helps those who help themselves" is contained somewhere within Holy Scripture. In actuality, this phrase comes from Ben Franklin,[6] and this way of understanding God and humanity was one of the first to be condemned as heresy by the Christian church.

Unlike Pelagianism, traditional Christianity does not say we get what we deserve based on our effort or merits. It offers, instead, a completely different logic. In our relationships with other human beings and the world, we often get less than we deserve. In our relationship with God, we are consistently offered grace, a free gift from God that is more than we deserve and is in no way owed to us. This gift of grace is God's doing, not ours, and it is the only context in which the concept of sin makes any sense at all. Sin can only be known after grace has been given. It is only in the context of God's love for us that our turning away from God in sin is understood to be wrong, self-distorting, and deadly. God's grace comes first.

This is the heart of Augustine's response to Pelagius: an insistence on the priority of God's grace. God's grace must come first. In theological parlance this is called "prevenient" grace. Note that the logic runs from grace to sin and not the other way around. Augustine reasoned that since we baptize infants, affirming and conferring the grace of God, all humans must be sinful from the beginning. If Pelagianism were correct and humanity could manage to avoid sin by our own efforts, Christ would have died in vain.[7] In this context, Augustine argues that the sin of Adam and Eve was transmitted to all of humanity such that we are fallen and cannot choose good on our own. Evil is powerful; sin is universal. Without grace, we will always and only sin. This echoes the Pauline affirmation that since God offers universal grace in Jesus Christ, humanity must have collectively fallen in the sin of Adam.

There is a clear shift in Augustine's thought over time. In his earlier writings against Manichaeism, he emphasizes the freedom and responsibility of human beings in choosing to sin. In his later writings against Pelagianism, he emphasizes the pervasive power of sin and the human inability to choose the good apart from grace. There are scriptural roots to both views, and each can be found highlighted in later Christian traditions.[8] Many scholars change their minds over time, and to some degree the shift in Augustine's thought is just another example of this noble tradition. However, in another way, the two views of Augustine, when held together, represent the paradoxical way in which much of the Christian tradition speaks of sin. We are free and responsible, and we cannot get out of this mess on our own. We do make choices and should make good ones. Yet even when we know the good, we often cannot do it. We are free and we are slaves, responsible for our decisions and yet in bondage to sin. To many who did not grow up within Christianity, this seems like nonsense and contradiction, yet many Christians recognize this as a true account of our condition.

Freedom and responsibility are often much more complex than equally possible choices between good and bad options. Consider, for example, an alcoholic. There is ample evidence that some people have a genetic predisposition for becoming an alcoholic, and that environmental factors involved in growing up as the child of an alcoholic play a role in fostering alcoholism. Furthermore, certain life experiences or circumstances (notably, in our present circumstances, returning home from a long tour of combat duty) correlate to higher incidence of alcoholism. Such evidence means that it is possible to identify certain groups of individuals as being at increased risk of becoming alcoholics long before the individuals in question take a drink. Once a person chooses to start drinking and then succumbs to alcoholism, freedom is further complicated. Often an alcoholic knows that she should not drink and, indeed, deeply desires to stop drinking. No one forces her to drink—she can always choose not to pick up the bottle. She is free not to drink and responsible for her actions. Yet she may well find herself echoing the words of Paul, "I do not do what I want, but I do the very thing I hate" (Rom. 7:15). There is a kind of bondage in addiction: the will is not free to choose the good. At the same time, every day many alcoholics in recovery choose not to drink again.

Obviously, this is an inexact analogy that has many flaws. For example, Christians cannot recover from sin in such a way that we do not do it anymore, while an alcoholic in recovery can actually stop drinking. I use this analogy merely to illuminate the paradox that humans are both responsible for sin and in bondage to it, that sin is both our own misuse of freedom and a force larger than ourselves. For many people the concrete example of alcoholism is more familiar than the early and late writings of Augustine.[9]

From the Bible and from theologians and communities struggling with the issue since then, the Christian tradition has developed a view of sin as a turning away from right relation with God that distorts the entire human person. Sin is both an individual matter, as it concerns the actions of specific people in their own freedom, and a communal affair, since we all, from the earliest beginnings of humanity, are involved and implicated in sin. Sin is deeply rooted in human freedom. At the same time, it is more than just the cumulative account of negative choices made by human beings. When sin entered into the world, something of great value to humanity was lost or damaged, and as a result our freedom was compromised. We are in bondage to sin, and we are in need of grace. Indeed, it is only through the lens of grace that sin can be seen truly, and it is always in the context of grace that sin must be understood.

Contemporary Views

Up to this point I have been speaking as if there were a single view of sin within Christianity. Yet throughout this book I have emphasized that Christianity is a multiple and fluid tradition, such that many different Christian theologies flourish in different times, places, and communities. I attempted to make my comments about sin above so general that they would cover most of the various specific views of this doctrine that have been influential in mainstream Christianity in the West. Please note, however, that other views within Christianity have been excluded or marginalized for the purpose of making some basic characteristics of the dominant view clear. In the pages that follow, I will speak more specifically about three ways of looking at the doctrine of sin that are vital in contemporary theology: Reformed Protestant, Roman Catholic, and liberation. While this discussion will be more particular and nuanced than the background section above, it is still wildly generalized. Any single theologian will no doubt differ significantly from the typology I offer here, and these three categories do not begin to cover the totality of Christian traditions operative today. I recognize, and emphasize, the limitations of the generalizing overview that I describe. At the same time, I believe that a rough typology of differing views can be concretely useful in understanding the specific perspectives of different Christian communities.

The three types of views on sin that I will describe here are not parallel, for the first two (Roman Catholic and Protestant) represent specific Christian groups that can be located in different churches on any given Sunday. The third, liberation, refers not to a specific denominational group or church, but rather to a way of thinking that began among Roman Catholics and now flourishes among Christians in many different denominations, churches, and sects. I will begin by describing Roman Catholic and Reformed Protestant views of sin and then introduce the liberation theology movement and the ways it has influenced and nuanced both of these.

The tricky bit about putting Roman Catholic and Reformed Protestant theologies side by side is maintaining a balanced view of just how small yet significant the differences between the two are. They are like twin sisters whose differences of temperament stand out more starkly because their features are so similar. Roman Catholic and Reformed Christians both tell the same Christian story: God desires to be in loving communion with God and so created the universe. Humans are created in God's image. We sin. God reveals Godself. Jesus, the incarnation of God, comes to be with us in his life and ministry, is executed on a cross, and is raised from the dead. The Christ event enables the relationship between God and humanity to move forward toward its ultimate culmination in the new creation. God continues to be present with us in the church and through the Holy Spirit, and we should respond to God's grace by loving God and neighbor. All the major plot points are the same for these two strands of Christian tradition.

However, the emphasis is very different between the two. In the modern period, one can describe this story in Roman Catholic theology as having a nature-grace dynamic. God graces us in creation and with a nature that is made in the image of God. Over time and in history, God continues to bestow grace on us that is fitting to who we are, such that the story unfolds as grace upon grace, moving ever closer to full communion between humanity and the Divine. In contrast, in the modern period, the Reformed story has a sin-redemption dynamic. The center of the story is the tragic tale of our rejection of God and the dramatic Jesus event that heals this awful breach. Note that Reformed Christians also speak of grace upon grace, but it is a side plot. Likewise, Roman Catholics speak of sin and redemption, but this is a (highly significant) side plot that must be understood in terms of the larger dramatic arc of nature and grace. The story is the same; the flavor is different.[10]

Roman Catholic Views of Sin

A Roman Catholic doctrine of sin takes place within a nature-grace framework in which the major story line is God's desire to be in loving relationship with humanity.[11] God creates us as human in the image of God. In a fitting unfolding of the beginning grace of creation, God acts in human history, continues to offer yet more grace, and eventually comes to be with us in Jesus Christ. In Jesus, through the Holy Spirit, God offers to each of us a future of beatific vision, an eternity of divine communion. We have a measure of freedom and dignity that—when it is enabled by the prevenient grace of God—permits us to choose, in our turn, to accept God's offer of salvation and be in loving relation with God. God saves us. We do not save ourselves through good behavior or meritorious acts. Yet God chooses to save us in a way that respects our freedom and dignity, allowing us (and enabling us, through grace) to participate in our own salvation by accepting God's offer. We accept this offer in many ways, primarily in a faith that is enacted in community through love of God and love of neighbor. Within this major plotline, the turning away of humanity in sin is our rejection of God's offer, our unthinkable, impossible saying no to grace. In the event of Jesus Christ, God keeps saying yes to us despite our communal no, in such a way that God's desire to be in loving relationship with humanity is guaranteed to triumph. In the one person Jesus Christ, humanity says yes to God's offer, establishing an eternal communion of human and divine. This means that even though we continue to sin, through the grace given in Jesus, we can say yes to God's permanent offer of salvation.

Earlier I noted both that sin is rooted in human freedom and that humans are in bondage to sin. Another way of saying this is that sin is both something we do and a condition in which we find ourselves. These two aspects of human sin are affirmed by both Roman Catholic and Reformed Christians, yet there is, I believe, a difference in emphasis. Again noting that this is a painful generalization, within contemporary Roman Catholicism, sin is viewed primarily as an *act*. It is something you do or neglect to do. Each person in the community is commanded by God to live in a certain way. While we have different abilities to live up to these ideals, we each are held accountable to what we are capable of doing. This means that a six-year-old is not expected to act with the same ethical and spiritual wherewithal as a forty-year-old. We each are required to do the right thing to the degree that we are able. The institutional church has been reflecting on the behavioral standards for Christians for nearly two thousand years, so there is quite a bit of history, quite a number of rules to live by. However, and this is extremely important to remember, the ultimate guide for each Roman Catholic is his or her own conscience. Imagine that the pope were to issue an infallible decree tomorrow saying that all Catholics should do X. Roman Catholic theology demands that any Catholic who (with prayer, study, and reflection) could not do X in good conscience should not do so. Individual conscience, faithfully examined in conversation with the tradition and community, trumps.

Note that this description of sin is both very individual, since it is about individual freedom, capacity, and conscience, and very communal. The guidelines for behavior have been worked out in community over time. Furthermore, sin is seen as something that upsets the equilibrium of the community in which we all live.[12] A sin against God is a sin against the community, and vice versa. Also, sin itself is a characteristic of the entire community. Sin is a communal reality that affects each of us from our very beginnings, at least in the form of original sin.

Roman Catholic theologian Karl Rahner describes original sin as the loss of original righteousness. Before sin, the desires, powers, and affections of the human person were aligned by right relation to God. We were held together, and smoothly functioning, by a particularly gracious relationship of mutual love between creature and Creator. In freely turning away from God as our own highest good, humanity lost the organizing and aligning effects of original righteousness. Without this aligning grace of mutual loving relationship with God, we are profoundly tempted to sin. We freely, but virtually inevitably, choose to turn away from God. Individual human freedom is always enacted within finitude, history, and community. This means that we are not absolutely free, but only relatively so. Our choices are affected by our circumstances, influenced by the world around us in innumerable ways. Since sin entered the picture and original righteousness was lost, each human being born into the world has entered a situation in which his or her freedom is partially determined by the sinful choices made by others in the human community. This is original sin. Thus in Rahner's theology, original sin is not seen as the shared debt, inherited guilt, or dirty beginnings of humanity.[13] Instead, it is the situation in which our free choices are influenced by the sin and guilt of others throughout human history, which comes to be through the loss of original righteousness. In this situation of original sin, we will invariably choose to sin, engaging in actual sin and thereby bringing our own personal guilt on ourselves.

Another way to think about original righteousness and original sin is this: If there were no sin, we would be both *pulled* forward into loving communion with God by the coming grace of the new creation, inaugurated in Jesus Christ, and *pushed* forward into this communion by the collective weight, habits, and influence of a human history filled with loving relation to God. Since sin has entered the picture, we are pulled forward by God, but our own human history is a mixed bag. It does not unequivocally propel us toward divine communion, but rather it places us in temptation and instills in us a propensity to sin.[14]

A caveat is needed. Throughout this description, and at different points in this chapter, I speak as if there were a chronological sequence of innocent beginnings, followed by a first, temporal sin, followed by our current situation. This is for convenience and clarity. The story of Adam and Eve, the drama of the fall, contains such useful and powerful symbolism that it is difficult to abandon it. However, please note that the vast majority of contemporary Christian theologians do not read this story literally or imagine a temporal past of perfect purity in the garden. Instead, the narration of original righteousness, or life before the fall, is an account of our sense of what humanity is meant to be, of the gracious intent of the Creator. The dramatic arc of innocence, temptation, sin, and fallen state provides a symbolic framework for expressing the Christian conviction (known only through grace) that we are not now as we were meant to be.

What does the dynamic of sin and grace look like in the life of a Catholic Christian? What does this type of theology of sin offer? First, it offers explanation. On the most general level, doctrines of sin help explain a world of suffering, evil, and nastiness. They help us to affirm that creation is good and that humanity is good, even though the evidence points in the other direction. They help us to acknowledge the depth and breadth of our own wrongdoing and the disastrous consequences. More specifically, Roman Catholic views of sin tell a truth about who we are: we have freedom that we cannot avoid—we must make choices. God helps us know—through conscience, revelation, and community—basic guidelines for good behavior. These guidelines are not just about morals or ethics, but also fundamentally about living in right relation with

God and our community. And even though we are free and (often) know what we should do, we often mess up. We consistently turn from God and neighbor. Roman Catholic theologies of sin hold us accountable for our behavior and call us on our misdeeds. My youngest son is four years old, and I find myself saying to him, "You know better!" This is both a reprimand for his naughtiness and a reminder that he is a person of dignity and some measure of reason whom I respect enough to expect him to behave well. Roman Catholic theology does something similar for us.

Then, when we recognize that we are not being (or becoming) whom we are called to be, we can come to the church, to the community, and tell the truth of who we are from our perspective. We can confess all that we have done wrong, repent of the harm we have inflicted on our community, and be recalled into right relations. We are granted relief. Through the rituals of confession, penance, and absolution, we can be reconciled with God and our community. We are enfolded back into our community and reminded that the most basic truth of who we are is that we are children of God. We are, first and foremost, good. We are created in the image of God, who loves us. It is true that we are sinners. But this is not the final, most fundamental truth of who we are. We are those to whom God offers God's own self as our grace-filled future. By grace, in freedom, we can accept that offer.

Reformed Protestant Views of Sin

A Reformed Protestant (I use this phrase to refer to those Protestant congregations that have roots in the work of Reformers such as Luther and Calvin) understanding of sin takes place within a sin-redemption model, in which the major story line is our rejection of God in sin and God's work to heal this breach in the event of Jesus Christ. God's desire for loving communion with humanity, the grace of creation, and the fulfillment of this desire in the new creation form the essential backdrop against which the drama of sin and redemption makes sense. Originally in a covenant relationship of mutual love with God, humanity broke the covenant by turning away from God. In so doing, we became tainted and distorted by sin. Both finite and sinful, we can do nothing to redeem ourselves or right the situation. Through the event of Jesus Christ, God both condemns our sinfulness and acts on our behalf to restore us to right relationship with God. We are declared justified by God; therefore, we are truly made right with God. Yet this is not a result of our own works or the consequence of a change within ourselves. Rather, it is the work of a loving God who freely chooses to love us and to enact that love salvifically in Jesus. We remain sinners even after we are justified, such that we are *simul iustus et peccator* (justified and sinners at the same time). Our salvation is entirely wrought by God; we play no part in making it happen. However, when we are given the gift of faith, we are called to respond joyfully to God's grace with love of God and love of neighbor.

Recalling that human sin is both something we do and a condition in which we find ourselves, one can see the emphasis in Reformed Protestant theology on sin primarily as a *state*.[15] It is a mark of who we are after the fall. In sin the human person is profoundly distorted, such that not only do we have a propensity to do the wrong thing, but we are incapable of doing the right thing or clearly knowing the difference between the two. The classic example of how sin changes humanity in Reformed theology is that of ink and water. Imagine a glass of clear water. To this, add one drop of green ink. Within moments, there is no part of the water that is untainted. It is all green, all a distortion of its former self. It is still water, still H_2O, yet there is no drop untainted, no bit preserved pure. Similarly, once sin enters humanity, there is no part of us (either individually or communally) that is not distorted or tainted by sin. We are still human, but there is no pure reserve within humanity that can know or act without the influence of sin. This means that even the most righteous act of the most righteous person is still sinful. This is called total depravity. It does not mean there is no good left in us, but rather that no part of our fundamentally good structure is left untainted or untwisted by the effects of sin. The doctrine of total depravity means that we really cannot do anything to help ourselves, because every effort we make on our own behalf will be further sin. We cannot do right by following our own conscience or the guidelines of the church—both of these are deeply tainted by sin. The condition of original sin leads inevitably and inexorably to actual sin. We cannot say yes to God's offer of salvation; we will always say no. Therefore, we must depend entirely on the grace of God.

This view of sin is both individual and communal, but in a different way than the Roman Catholic view. Each human person is distorted by sin, and we all are in the same boat together. This ink-stained state of total depravity is original sin. Out of it will necessarily arise actual sin. Each one of us will choose to sin. While Reformed Protestants parse freedom differently than Catholics, there is still a sense of culpability here. We are in bondage to sin, such that we cannot will the good, yet we are still responsible for our own fall. We do not have the freedom required to participate in our own salvation, and sin is more a tragic state than a specific, freely chosen negative action, but sin itself still has origins in the misuse of human freedom. On a daily basis, we must make choices, and our choices are never without sin.

What does the dynamic of sin and grace look like in the life of a Reformed Protestant Christian? What does this type of theology of sin offer? At first, the whole scheme might seem quite harsh. Yet it has extraordinary explanatory power. On a large scale, it helps explain why even when we are trying our best to do the right thing, we always muck it up. Even our humanitarian efforts betray a deep-seated, often unconscious self-interest. This is not just about our actions, but also about our knowledge. While our ways of acting tend to benefit us, our ways of knowing tend to put ourselves at the center of all things, distorting our vision of the world. On a more individual level, this is something I can see quite clearly in myself. My own motives are never pure. Earlier today I stopped to talk with the homeless woman who sells flowers, buying two carnations and asking about her day. If I attempt rigorous honesty, I recognize that some part of me was proud of being a good person for giving her money, and some even less desirable part of me was hoping that one of my academic colleagues might be impressed that I am on a first-name basis with the flower lady.

Thus the Reformed Protestant doctrine of sin also tells the truth of who we are. In this view, our deepest, darkest secrets and worst fears of our inadequacy are confirmed. Yes, we really are a thorough mess. The worst that we are and can be is known by God, and every bit of us falls short of God's glory. Before God we have nothing to argue in our own defense but must accept judgment as sinful creatures. The hard part to put in words here is the enormous relief that comes from that. We are fully known by God, and we cannot help ourselves, so we can stop our constant efforts to justify our own existence. It is not up to us to make our lives worth living or to make ourselves people God could love. We have no resources for these tasks. Precisely when we realize we don't have a leg to stand on, we end up on our knees, asking for the grace of God. And there we find acceptance and love. God knows exactly who we are and is not glossing over the bad bits. We are condemned and convicted. Yet we are also taken up into the grace of Jesus Christ, accepted by God as beloved children. We do not have to justify our own lives. God does that. We do not have to make ourselves lovable. God loves us. It is not up to us to create the value of our existence; that job has been accomplished by the Creator of the universe, and our consistent efforts to destroy it have been reversed by Jesus Christ.

Such relief is profoundly liberating and generates a disposition of responsible joy. Someone who has experienced this dynamic of grace can look at every other person in the world and know that we all, equally, are sinners in the eyes of God. And yet, as we have been granted undeserved forgiveness, we should treat all those we encounter with forbearance, generosity, and humility. The Reformed Protestant view of sin does not demand right behavior but inspires it. Of course, even the actions of a faithful Christian will be sinful. But this does not inhibit action. Instead, even our own sinfulness is entrusted into the grace of God, and we offer our best efforts for God's purposes. When it comes to our attempts to respond to God's grace with love for God and neighbor, we should, in the words of Martin Luther, "sin boldly. And trust in the love of God more boldly still."[16]

These two rough sketches of Catholic and Reformed views of sin should not be set in stark opposition. The differences between them, while real and important, should not be overstated. Roman Catholics speak of sin as a state when speaking of original sin and can see much wisdom in the Protestant account of fallen humanity. Some contemporary Roman Catholic theologians affirm, in a nuanced way, that Christians are simultaneously justified and sinners. Likewise, Protestant theologians recognize the value of speaking of specific acts as sinful and can value the ethical imperatives and moral norms of a Roman Catholic view.[17]

A Liberation Theology View of Sin

Liberation theology is a way of doing theology that emerged among Roman Catholics in Latin America in the 1960s. Since then it has been influential in many countries and among many different Christian groups, such that today there are liberation theologies from many distinct traditions. There are Catholic liberation theologians (such as Gustavo Gutiérrez) and Reformed Protestant liberation theologians (such as Letty Russell) as well. Liberation theology is defined not by denomination or church distinctions, but rather by a particular methodology, or way of doing theology. First, liberation theology is a process of both action and reflection. It is not a purely academic exercise that can be accomplished, start to finish, in the library. Liberation theology is done in the context of struggle for liberation of the poor and the oppressed. Second, liberation theology takes the experience of the poor seriously. The visions of God explicated by privileged academics in traditional Christian theology are not the only perspectives on God. There is much to learn from the insights of those who have been marginalized by society, whose wisdom has often been excluded from the theological tradition. Phillip Berryman writes that liberation theology is "an interpretation of Christian faith out of the experience of the poor . . . [and] an attempt to help the poor interpret their own faith in a new way."[18] Third, liberation theology affirms "the preferential option for the poor." This is by no means a valorization of poverty. Instead, it is reiteration of the Christian tradition's declaration that God cares for the poor and oppressed—caring for their needs has a privileged position in the Christian tradition. It also reflects the belief that God might look different from the position of the poor. Perhaps if we are not so invested in the status quo that grants us privilege, we can be more open to seeing the liberating action of God. These methodological commitments lead liberation theologies from various communities to have some common characteristics, such as depictions of God as liberator and visions of salvation that include physical, social, and spiritual well-being.

The various liberation theologies that have emerged in the last fifty years have deeply influenced how sin is understood by Catholics and Protestants alike. First, the liberation theology practice of doing theology "from the underside of history" shifts some of the pressing questions. In some circumstances, the reality that a community is sinned against might demand more reflection than the truth that we all are sinners. Second, liberation theologies have offered an account of sin as institutional, structural, and systemic, reconceptualizing the relationship between individual and communal sinfulness. Certain social structures, such as racism, are sinful. They have been created over time through the sinful choices of individuals and communities, and in turn they shape and influence individuals and communities. We all are deeply involved in social structures—from global capitalism to homophobic churches—that privilege some people over others, that harm members of our community, and that subtly or blatantly deny the image of God in those who are oppressed.

This view of sin as structural and institutional has enormous and persuasive explanatory power. It resonates deeply with elements of the Christian tradition—sin is both the misuse of freedom in the individual and something more, a pervasive power in the universe beyond individual freedom. Original sin can be easily understood through this lens. We each are born into a society that is already sinfully structured. Whether we are born with silver spoons in our mouths or on the wrong side of the tracks, we are already embedded in a sinful economic structure that harms some for the benefit of others, that neglects the poor and oppressed, and that profoundly limits and distorts our freedom. We cannot simply choose to opt out of these sinful structures; we are bound by them. On a daily basis, I reap the privileges and rewards of being white, heterosexual, and middle class. Were I to give away all that I own and walk away from my family, I would still carry those privileges with me, in the ways that I speak as an educated person, in the preferential treatment that whites receive in America, in the absence of the fear of homophobic hate crimes. Yet as we are bound in these structures, we also are called, by and with the grace of God, to freely resist them and work for their undoing.

Note here that liberation theology understandings of sin hold close together the realities of sin as something we do and a condition in which we find ourselves. On the one hand, sin is a state that we cannot escape. It shapes and taints all of our actions, our ways of knowing, our very being in the world. An innocent trip to the grocery store implicates us in the plight of migrant workers, the destruction of the earth through chemical farming methods, and the political and military struggles supported by our reliance on oil to bring produce from California to New Haven. On the other hand, sin is an action for which we are responsible. We do know better. We should do better. We are called to be in a different relationship with the world around us, not merely to accept this fallen state. In some ways, it is merely a further explication of the tension that has been present in Christian reflections on sin from the beginning. It stems from our freedom; we are in bondage.

Like both Reformed and Catholic views of sin, liberation views offer explanatory power and tell the truth about us—they convict us in ways that we can see and understand. Yet where is the relief here? Precisely because liberation theologies view sin as both state and act, it can seem that we are in an impossible bind—we cannot stop sinning, and we must stop sinning. This points to a risk in liberation theology. It can offer conviction without relief, guilt without absolution, condemnation without acceptance. Insofar as it requires us to step into the struggle for liberation and use our own efforts to make this world a better place before we can have our clearest view of God, liberation theology can seem like a new form of Pelagianism, in which we act first and experience grace second.

Yet, at its best, it does not do this. One of the fundamental insights of liberation theology is that Christianity is not just something to be believed; it is something to be lived. The affirmation that we are called to act, to struggle for liberation, does not mean that our action comes before God's grace. Liberation theologies most often describe human action as a response to grace, either as a grace-enabled acceptance of God's offer of salvation or as a joyous response to God's gracious bestowal of new life and a vision of new creation. Most liberation theologians are committed to a particular Christian tradition, and therefore they describe sin and the response to it in ways that rely more heavily on either Catholic or Protestant theologies. The Roman Catholic liberation theologian Gustavo Gutiérrez describes our accepting God's grace through love of neighbor in the struggle for liberation.[19] The Reformed Protestant liberation theologian Letty Russell casts the struggle for liberation as an opportunity to live into the good news of salvation, anticipating the new creation that has already been inaugurated in Jesus Christ.[20] Thus liberation theology can offer the same kinds of relief that are present in Catholic and Reformed views.

At the same time, through its emphasis on theology as both reflection and action, liberation theology can offer one more element. Christian responses to grace are not merely internally or intellectually appropriated. They are enacted, performed, and lived in the world. Within the purview of liberation theology, when a Christian, through grace, comes to respond to the conviction of sin by struggling for the liberation of the poor and oppressed, she or he can experience a particular kind of profound relief in that activity. There are a couple of ways I can think of to explain this, both of which fall far short of capturing this experience, no doubt in part because I do not spend most of my days in the struggle for liberation. First, for those of us who fall more on the oppressor than oppressed side of things, action in solidarity with the oppressed can be a form of repentance in which we ask to be received back into the very community that we have harmed. I once attended a *campesina* mass in Nicaragua. I had expected to be greeted there by people who would hate me as an American, since America had done so much damage to this country in the 1980s, up to and including the Iran-Contra affair. Instead, they were welcoming. They did not deny the harm done but offered hospitality to any American who did not deny or ignore the terrorist activities of the American government on our behalf. I was embraced by the community that I had, by my mere existence as an American, participated in damaging. As we walked to receive the Eucharist, I prayed with those around me, "Lord, I am unworthy to receive you, but say the word and I will be made whole." This was a profound experience of grace in my life.

The second way I will try to explain the experience of relief from sin that can come from struggling for the poor and oppressed comes from a novel that does not speak explicitly about Christianity at all. In *Animal Dreams*, author Barbara Kingsolver describes two sisters choosing different paths during the 1980s. Hallie, a plant specialist, moves to Nicaragua to help the revolutionaries who are trying to feed the people under attack by the Contras. Codi, back home in America, is afraid for her sister to be in such a dangerous place and feels guilty and inadequate because she is not devoting her life to helping others. Hallie writes to Codi explaining that she is not in Nicaragua to try to save the world. She writes:

> Codi, here's what I've decided: the very least you can do in your life is to figure out what you hope for. And the most you can do is live inside that hope. Not admire it from a distance but live right in it, under its roof. What I want is so simple I almost can't say it: elementary kindness. Enough to eat, enough to go around. The possibility that kids might one day grow up to be neither the destroyers nor the destroyed. That's

about it. Right now I'm living in that hope, running down its hallway and touching the walls on both sides.

I can't tell you how good it feels. I wish you knew. I wish you'd stop beating yourself up for being selfish and really *be* selfish. . . . I wish you knew how to squander yourself.[21]

I am not a liberation theologian. Instead, I am a middle-class working mother, constantly making compromises with my own complicity, pleased that my new car is a hybrid. I do not know firsthand the hope or the joy that Hallie describes. But I have spent enough time around liberation theologians that I have seen it before. I have seen them squander themselves, and I am convinced that it is palpable grace. There is a marked difference between action fueled by the urgent need to save the world and the self-squandering action that comes from a profound commitment to the good news that the salvation of the world is in the trustworthy hands of God. The best liberation theologies invite us all into the hallways of that hope.

The Wisdom of Sin

Each of these Christian ways of considering sin offers at least three benefits that are not easily found elsewhere. First, they help explain why a world of so much love and goodness is also filled with so much evil and pain. Any newspaper, on any given day, bears ample evidence of the dignity and kindness of humanity, as well as of our meanness and barbarity. A sturdy Christian doctrine of sin allows us to hold these truths together, acknowledging that we are children of God who are also deeply fallen. Second, Christian doc-trines of sin convict us. They tell the truth that we are profoundly messed up. We do not do the good we want; we want the wrong goods; we cannot even tell the good from the bad much of the time. In convicting us of all the many ways that we fall short of the glory of God, doctrines of sin tell us the truth about ourselves and hold us accountable to higher standards of behavior. Third, Christian doctrines of sin offer us relief. This is not the justice-dodging respite of a get-out-of-jail-free card or a panacea that says we are really okay. It is something much more. For Reformed Protestants, it is the relief of being fully and completely known, accepted, loved, and offered new life transformed by the grace of Jesus Christ. For Roman Catholics, it is the relief of not pretending, of being honest about who we are and being welcomed back into the community that we have harmed. It is the relief of being assured that we are children of God, called into communion with God, and that—for all our missteps—we are still on a journey of saying yes to the future God wills for us.

These benefits—explanation, conviction, and relief—can be hard to find in some contemporary Christian communities. They cannot be found in watered-down Christianity that teaches we can all be happy if we act the right way, pray the right way, and believe the right way. They cannot be found in militant Christianity that focuses all talk of sin on how those other, bad people live and what we must do to stop them, through condemnation, legislation, and clear delineation of who is in and who is out of God's favor. And these three benefits of Christian wisdom about sin are antithetical to contemporary American consumer culture—not just different, but truly opposed.

One of the most common descriptions of sin, beginning in the work of Augustine and used by both Protestants and Catholics later, is that sin is being curved inward on ourselves. Imagine, for a moment, how many American businesses rely on our inward-curvedness. In our daily lives we are barraged with advertisements and entertainments that narrate a twisted opposite of Christian doctrines of sin. We are told that we are wrong in every possible but superficial way. Our skin looks wrong, feels wrong, grows too much hair in some places and not enough in others, and the hair is all the wrong color anyway. We eat the wrong foods, wear the wrong clothes, own the wrong things. We are spending our time in all the wrong ways: we are not nearly productive enough, we are not doing things well enough, and it has been too long since our last vacation. At the exact same time that we are told how bad we are, we are also being told that we deserve more. We should have better skin, hair, food, things, lives. We should change our hair color because we are "worth it." The inherent paradox—you are a mess but you should fix it because you deserve better—often goes unnoticed. The good news of American consumerism is that all of your flaws can be hidden if you have enough money and buy the right products.

The three benefits of Christian doctrines of sin are not to be found in this consumer culture. This contemporary perversion of a doctrine of sin does not explain the world; it distracts us from it. It is hard to ponder global warming or the number of casualties in Iraq while walking through the mall. Consumer culture is an escape route from reality that might be useful in small doses but, over time and for a whole nation, fosters a state of culpable ignorance.

This story of who we are does not convict us. It does not begin to touch how bad we are or how good we are. The problems with humanity are more than skin deep. Calvinist theology, depicting the total depravity of humanity in contrast to the infinite divine glory, says we are a "stench in the nostrils of God." American consumer culture just tells us that we stink—our breath is bad, our armpits sweaty, our laundry stale. For those of us with an ounce of self-reflection, we know this is not the real truth of who we are. Our secrets are much more shameful and scarier than bodily imperfections or stylistic woes.

Neither does this story offer us relief. Consumer culture does not want to fix any of the issues it diagnoses as problems. If it offered a real solution, each person would be a one-time customer.

Instead, advertisers attempt to convince us to hide and disguise our failings, to constantly cover up our embarrassments with new applications of pricey products. This is not about being fully known by God or the community; it is about making sure that no one ever sees you as you truly are. The game here is to convince each of us that we are horribly wrong, but that we can hide this fact from everyone else. What is required of us to pull off this charade is constant vigilance. We can look better to the rest of the world, but only through ceaseless striving.

Nothing could be further from a Christian doctrine of sin. This narrative of who we are, which surrounds us in American consumer culture, is devoid of grace. I have emphasized in this chapter the traditional affirmation that sin is only known through grace. Here I am arguing that in offering us explanation, conviction, and relief, the wisdom of sin is itself a form of grace, a gift of God.

Grace and Sin
Shawnthea Monroe and Shannon Craigo-Snell

First, there is grace. That is where any discussion of the doctrine of sin should begin. Like the old hymn says, " 'Twas grace that taught my heart to fear, and grace those fears relieved." The grace of God is the merciful context in which we come to know ourselves as fallen creatures, people who have been created for better things. Once we apprehend who God is, what God has done for us in Jesus Christ, then there is a relationship in the context of which we can face our brokenness. In other words, it is only in the light of the goodness and glory of God that the degree to which we fall short of that glory is clear.

We understand sin to be a self-distorting turning away from the love of God. Here we agree with much of the Christian tradition, which describes sin as an inward-curvedness. This is precisely why the doctrine of sin is an inward-directed doctrine. It is a word for *us*—as individuals and faith communities—a theological claim that calls us to faithful and thorough self-reflection and self-correction. Yet, while it may be true that this doctrine is a God-given tool for our own betterment, we resist this inward journey. Mainline Christians tend to avoid the subject, confessing our debts and trespasses but rarely identifying ourselves as sinners. Other more conservative Christians have sometimes turned the doctrine of sin outward, using it as a tool to identify and criticize the "other." Nowhere else is this more apparent than in the way the Christian church approaches the issue of homosexuality.

With the exception of a handful of Scripture passages, the biblical witness is frustratingly silent on the subject of homosexuality. Even the word *homosexual* is a modern invention, inserted into contemporary translations as a way of unifying a diverse biblical understanding. It doesn't come up in the Ten Commandments or in any of Jesus' teachings. Admittedly, there is no scriptural support for homosexual relationships, but there's no clear biblical case against them either. And yet Christians of every stripe have relied upon Scripture to support the belief that homosexuality is a sin and that homosexuals, by extension, are sinners.

Some conservative Christians take the direct approach, declaring homosexuality a sin by quoting Leviticus 18:22, "You shall not lie with a man as with a woman; it is an abomination," or 1 Corinthians 6:9, where Paul identifies sodomites as among those who shall not inherit the kingdom. To be fair, Leviticus also lists shellfish as an abomination (Lev. 11:10), but apparently the patrons of Red Lobster do not fall under the judgment of the Lord. Paul's list of the condemned also includes adulterers, drunkards, and the greedy—three categories that cut a wide swath through contemporary American society—yet only homosexuals are condemned in the public discourse.[22]

Some mainline Christians take a subtler approach when it comes to the subject of homosexuality. They do not willingly call homosexuals sinners, but they passively allow homosexuality to be defined as sin. Here's how the logic works: The biblical definition of marriage found in Genesis states, "Then the man said, 'This at last is bone of my bones and flesh of my flesh; this one shall be called Woman, for out of Man this one was taken.' Therefore a man leaves his father and his mother and clings to his wife, and they become one flesh" (Gen. 2:23-24). From this piece of Scripture, the argument proceeds: marriage is a covenant between a man and a woman; any sexual relationship outside of marriage is a sin; therefore, because homosexuals cannot be married, any noncelibate homosexual relationship is sinful. It's a seemingly dispassionate line of logic that enables mainline Christians to welcome homosexuals into the life of the church but to exclude them from ordination and full participation in the life of the community. When challenged, we feign helplessness in the face of the irrefutable demands of Scripture.

Whether one takes the direct or indirect approach, the effect is the same. The doctrine of sin is projected outward onto others and becomes a tool of exclusion. Jesus warned the disciples specifically about this, asking, "Why do you see the speck in your neighbor's eye, but do not notice the log in your own eye?" (Matt. 7:3). The doctrine of sin is meant to be an acknowledgment of our *own* flaws in light of the grace of God.

A further danger in misusing the doctrine of sin is that by identifying others as sinners, we avoid addressing our own sinful behaviors. Let's return to the case of homosexuality. By focusing on the sexual orientation of a small part of the Christian community, we have kept ourselves from addressing the more pressing issue of Christian sexual ethics. Sexuality, like all other aspects of human life, can become an occasion for sin—an opportunity to turn away from the love of God—for people of all sexual orientations. A robust Christian ethic around human sexuality would make claims and demands upon us all.

It is fairly easy for Christians to fall into the trap of directing the doctrine of sin outward because there are times when we feel we must condemn the actions of other people. The impulse to condemn is not always a bad one. Indeed, it is important for Christian communities to name and reject behaviors that cause suffering and contribute to evil in the world. However, we are convinced that the theological impetus and justification for condemnation should never come from the doctrine of sin.

Grace comes first. It is grace that allows us to see when we fall short of the glory of God, when we break the bonds of covenant, and when we betray our identities as those whom God loves. The starting point for a Christian theological evaluation of any action must be grace. Does this action respond to the grace of God with gratitude and love? We must look first to the gifts of God and then examine our reception of these gifts.

For example, the doctrine of Christology explores the grace of God in Jesus Christ. Here we learn that Jesus identifies with the poor and the oppressed, honors the outcast, and includes the marginalized. He tends to the physical needs of those around him, healing the sick and feeding the hungry. He proclaims God's love for all persons. The grace we come to know in Jesus, then, warrants the condemnation of behaviors and systems that exploit the poor, marginalize categories of people, and make it more difficult for people's bodily needs to be met. Such harmful activities deny and reject the grace of God as revealed in Jesus Christ, and therefore can be named as sin.

In speaking of the goodness of God and God's love for humanity, there is room and requirement to identify what is wrong in the world and even, with care, to say that someone is doing something sinful. Yet such condemnations ought not begin with the doctrine of sin. Instead, they should stem from the acknowledgment of grace. The role of the doctrine of sin in such statements should be to remind Christians that we are all sinful. As sinners, we should be humble in our evaluation of others, knowing that our best judgments of what is and ought to be are always flawed and that our own behaviors are never purely righteous. The doctrine of sin is useful in naming sin and evil in the world around us because it constantly reminds us that self-righteousness is the home of the sinner, and whenever we occupy that territory, we too have gone astray.

"Warts and All"
Shawnthea Monroe

I once served a church that did not have a prayer of confession as part of the worship service. I asked the board of deacons why this was so, and they explained that they confessed their sins only during Lent. I responded that this was fine if that was the only time of year they sinned. When I suggested that we return to the practice of confessing our sins, I was accused of being old-fashioned and a fundamentalist. I was told that the congregation found confessing sins to be depressing and that it had a dampening effect on the joyful spirit of worship. One woman explained, "Confessing our sins is a downer."

She's right. Confessing our sins is a downer. Because if we confess our sins, that means we first must take an honest look at ourselves, and once we do that, it's hard not to get depressed. It's especially hard to do this in public. I'm not surprised that some people would rather not say a prayer of confession.

For those attuned to the rhythm and logic of Christian worship, the absence of confession might seem somewhat shocking. But I think I understand our resistance, and it originates in two places. First, some people take a "never let them see you sweat" approach to life. Look around and you'll see what I see—people who have a lot invested in appearing capable, competent, trustworthy, and strong. Most of us would never publicly air our shortcomings in our professional lives. Instead, we take the John Wayne approach: "Never apologize, never explain: it's a sign of weakness." Weakness in our culture is not an asset. In the same way, some of us avoid confessing our sins because we fear it will diminish us in the eyes of others, or worse, in the eyes of God.

Yet, as I gaze out on this congregation, I don't see many John Wayne Christians. Most of us have a different reason for avoiding sin talk and confession, and it has nothing to do with how others see us—but rather with how we see ourselves. This reticence comes from a different place, a second direction.

When I was an undergraduate at the University of Minnesota, there was a yearly event that marked the arrival of warm weather. This harbinger of spring was more dependable than the first robin and more colorful than the first crocus—it was the annual visit of Brother Jed.

Brother Jed was a traveling evangelist, a real fire-and-brimstone showman who would appear the first week of sunshine. He would set up shop at the top of the campus mall, and day after day he would work the crowds on Christ's behalf, testifying to the terrors of hell that awaited those who did not heed his warning. As throngs of students passed by on their way to class, Brother Jed would call out, accusing us of crimes and misdemeanors—with some disturbing accuracy, I'm sorry to say.

Some students took the whole week off to enjoy the Brother Jed show. They would sit in the sunshine and heckle him, chanting along with some of his signature phrases: "Cast into the lake of fire!" "Liars and thieves and for-ni-ca-tors!" "Washed in the blood of the Lamb!" There were also believers who came to listen, students who thought Brother Jed was a prophet of the Lord, a modern-day John the Baptist, and agreed with his assessment that most of the student body was going straight to hell. But the rest of us paused for only a moment, listening long enough to hear our sins named and ourselves condemned, before heading back to class.

I don't know what my classmates thought of Brother Jed's ministry. Perhaps they didn't appreciate his views on sin and salvation. As for me, I thought as far as judgment went, Brother Jed was an amateur. Sure, he knew his Bible, but he didn't know me. His vague accusations and charges of wrongdoing barely scratched the surface. Only I knew exactly what a failure I was.

Years later an experience with a confirmation class in my congregation revealed how common this internal sense of failure and judgment is. We were discussing the great commandment, specifically the call to "love your neighbor as yourself." I gave each of the students a piece of paper and asked them to list their talents and accomplishments on one side and their failures on the other. After ten minutes I collected the papers and was amazed by the responses. In nearly every case, the failure ledger was full, covered with a list of sins, mistakes, and regrets; but the accomplishments column held one or two entries at best.

After fifteen years in ministry, I have come to believe that most people have an internal "Brother Jed," an interior critic who berates us for our sins and failures. We hear that inner voice so clearly that we cannot bear to hear the same words spoken aloud, especially in church. We avoid speaking of sin because the wounds are too deep and no prayer of confession could ever plumb the depths of our brokenness.

The truth is that we know precisely how bad we are. Our sins are ever before us, and this knowledge breaks our hearts. It is a miracle, then, that we dare to show up in church at all, knowing what we know. Naming our sins aloud is asking too much.

But I'm here to tell you that no matter how painful or depressing it is, we need to face our brokenness and confess our sins at the beginning of worship. There are two good reasons for doing so. First, if we're ever going to deal with that internal "Brother Jed," we're going to need help. We can't do it alone.

Paul describes the conflict beautifully, the struggle between the reason and the will. We know what we should do, we know the right course of action, we know what Jesus would do—that's not a difficult question to answer. But the *doing* is so hard. Paul, that great apostle and theologian of the church, said, "I do not understand my own actions. I don't know why I do these things!" How many of us, deep in the night, have asked the same question? *Why did I do that?* Faced with all our errors, we become nothing more than the sum of our failures. Our inability to do the right thing is a terrible burden—we tremble under its weight. But experience tells us we cannot do the right thing on our own.

So Jesus shows up, and he asks us to shift burdens. That is what he's talking about in this passage from Matthew. He's saying to us, "I know you are struggling. I know the weight of the burden you carry. Set it down." Jesus asks us to set down our burdens and trade them for something else—the yoke of Christ. This is the yoke of the one who understands what we have done and says, "There is more to you than that." "Come unto me, all you that are weary and are carrying heavy burdens, and I will give you rest. Take my yoke upon you, and learn from me; for I am gentle and humble in heart, and you will find rest for your souls. For my yoke is easy, and my burden is light" (Matt. 11:28-30). We can't do this by ourselves. That's why Jesus shows up.

Of course, most of us are doing our best, trying to solve the problem on our own. We're reading books, going to therapy, doing everything we can to make ourselves feel better. That reminds me of something I once heard Anne Lamott say: "The cracks are where the light gets in, but most of us are spackling like crazy." Friends, it's time to stop spackling. That's what Paul is saying.

And there's another reason for us to speak about sin and confess our sins before God: we're not revealing anything that God doesn't already know. The purpose of the prayer of confession is not to surprise the Lord with all our shocking failures. The purpose of confession is so that we stop fooling ourselves. Augustine said it best: "Before God can deliver us, we must undeceive ourselves." Confessing our sins does not bring about a change in God—it brings about a change in us. Only when we confess our sins are we able to receive what God has been trying to give us.

It sounds easy, doesn't it—facing and naming our sins? But it's not. It's rather harrowing—just as harrowing as shopping for clothes. Don't laugh! Clothes shopping is one of the scariest things I do. To get through the ordeal, I have a set of rules I follow. First, I always shop on an empty stomach. Second, I avoid cheap stores that have those fluorescent lights in the changing rooms that add twenty pounds and make the veins in my legs stand out. And most important, I never face the mirror until I am fully dressed, because if I get a peek at myself in the buff, I'm likely to flee the store, never to return. Only once I am fully clothed can I look in the mirror and make a decision. I know I'm not the only one who feels this way—admit it!

I think we feel the same way about our souls. If we can't face what we look like on the outside, how can we face what we look like on the inside? Truth be told, we don't want to know ourselves fully, and the suggestion that God knows us completely is a frightening thought.

But have courage; there is good news. And the good news is this: God loves us not the way we're supposed to be, not the way we could be, not the way we would be if only we showed some discipline and perseverance and read the Bible and prayed a little more. No, God loves us as we are now . . . and also loves us too much to leave us here.

When we confess our sins, we are just telling the truth about ourselves. We are broken. We are sinful. We are incapable of doing the right thing on our own. That's who we are—but not all we are. The real power of confession is that when we name our sins and set them down before God, then and only then can we hear what God says about us: we are beloved and made for good things. Then and only then can we take up the yoke of Christ and find peace and rest for our souls.

Yes, sin talk can bring you down. But that's when God can lift you up.

Four

Church

Why Ecclesiology Matters: The Question of Silver
Shawnthea Monroe

Not long ago a dispute broke out in my congregation among some of the women of the church. The disagreement arose in the course of planning a reception for a guest minister. The cause of the dispute? Silver. Let me explain. Our church is one of those historic beauties, nestled in the midst of a lovely community. Like so many urban churches, our congregation was once the spiritual home of the well-to-do and powerful. While those days have faded somewhat, some artifacts remain—especially the silver. Our silver closet is a repository for a staggering assortment of trays, tea sets, punch bowls, and utensils. To women of an older generation, these pieces are an important part of our history, used to mark special occasions. To younger women, they are simply serving pieces from a bygone era and, like white gloves, hopelessly old-fashioned and difficult to clean. The question was, should we use the good silver or not?

At the planning meeting, each side made its case. The president of the Women's Fellowship said it would be an insult to host a guest pastor without bringing out the silver. "We are known for our receptions and the gracious hospitality we extend." A young mother in her thirties who was chair of the planning committee countered, "But hospitality is about more than setting a table with silver. It's too much trouble to use those pieces anyway. A church is more than its silver." The discussion went on and on without resolution. Even after the meeting, it was clear that the question of silver had caused a division in the community. Pondering my role as pastor in this dispute, I wondered, *Is this what the church has come to—fights over silver?*

What I needed in that moment was a good doctrine of ecclesiology. Day-to-day life in the church can be episodic and frustrating for a pastor, even without silver. There are so many demands on a pastor's time—meetings to attend, sermons to write, mission projects to promote, Bible studies to lead, and parishioners to visit. I may start the day with a grand plan for furthering the kingdom, but I'm usually one phone call away from chaos. And every church has its unique challenges. Some churches lose their edge and slip into a comfortable holding pattern, unwilling to change or grow. Some churches are torn by conflict caused by clashes over personalities or doctrines or details. Some churches are just trying to survive, grieving the loss of the good old days. There are even some churches whose success overtakes the ministry. Without a narrative arc, some larger story to help structure and give meaning to everyday tasks, ministry can become a series of disconnected encounters.

Ecclesiology is the overarching story that gives shape to life in the church—for pastors as well as parishioners. Having a clearly articulated sense of the purpose of the church and how it works allows the Christian community to sort through everyday issues and competing demands, and compels Christians to pursue God's mission. And a robust ecclesiology can enable pastors to identify the operative theology at work in church conflicts. Furthermore, if the pastor does not provide a congregation with a theologically informed understanding of the church, the people will turn to whatever is at hand to help them make sense of their life as a Christian community. It could be social action, it could be the music program, it could be the fellowship, it could even be the silver. In the absence of a clear rationale for being the church, people will fill in the blanks.

All doctrines have a history, perhaps none more so than the doctrine of ecclesiology. Over the centuries, ecclesiology has developed primarily in response to crises and challenges from within the church and from outside the Christian community. Each theological challenge has led to a further articulation of what the church is—and is not. This advancing specificity has given rise in turn to a multiplicity of ecclesiologies—that is, there is no one theological understanding of *church*; there are dozens. If I were to graph the development of the doctrine of ecclesiology, it would look like a river delta, with one main channel dividing over and over until it becomes a multitude of small streams.

As a result, it is difficult to give a general description of ecclesiology. Instead, I find it is helpful to pick one path and follow it to the end, exploring how a particular theological understanding of *church* shapes and challenges life in a Christian community. My theologian of choice is Karl Barth, who outlined his ecclesiology in *Church Dogmatics*.[1]

Like every aspect of Barth's theology, his ecclesiology is grounded in his understanding of the person of Jesus Christ. Whatever we believe about the church is revealed in Jesus. Barth develops this doctrine by examining the four marks of the church, as set out in the Nicene Creed.[2] "We believe in the one holy catholic and apostolic church." Barth takes each of these marks—one, holy, catholic, apostolic—and interprets them in a distinctly Reformed Protestant way.

Before I discuss the specifics of Barth's ecclesiology, however, it is necessary to say a word about his general understanding of what the church is. Imagine human history as a line moving forward. This line is marked by sin until the arrival of Jesus, when God alters the course of the world. Post-Easter, human history moves forward toward the anticipated second coming, never losing sight of the empty tomb. In Pauline theology this is the "already" and the "not yet." According to Barth, the church exists only in this middle period, post-Easter but pre-return, and her sole purpose is to be the body of Christ. More specifically, those who constitute the church are, by definition, people who stand under the verdict of the cross revealed in the resurrection. They acknowledge what has been done by God in Jesus Christ. They also acknowledge Jesus as Lord. And in everything the church does, there is a reflexive theological move. We proclaim what has happened (the resurrection) and anticipate what is yet to come (the return) in unity with Christ. Until Christ returns, we are the church.

Barth is very clear that the church has no identity apart from what it is doing in the present moment. In other words, the church *is*. There is no essence apart from existence, no general understanding of "church." Another way to think of it is that *church* is a verb, not a noun. This keeps the church on her toes, ever aware of the requirement to be the body of Christ in every place and time. Yes, there is historical continuity, and what we do (who we are) as the church today is connected to what the church has done in the past, but this history does not trace through any institution but through the person of Jesus Christ. With that said, let us now turn to Barth's interpretation of the four marks of the church.

The Church Is One

The church in every place and time is held together and animated by the Holy Spirit. This is what makes her the church, the body of Christ. As it is the same Spirit who animates every congregation, so there is only one church. There can be no division in the one body. In reality there is much disunity and division among Christian communities. Barth would suggest that this is not a sign of God's intended diversity, but a symptom of our sinfulness.[3] If we were truly obedient to the Spirit, all divisiveness would cease.

Addressing Christian divisions, John Calvin found it necessary to make a distinction between the visible and invisible church. According to Calvin, the visible church is the earthly body of believers, saints as well as sinners. But there is also an invisible church composed of God's elect—both those in the world and those who have died. This invisible church is an eschatological promise, an object of hope for believers, even as believers must live out this hope in the flawed and sometimes divisive life of the visible church.[4]

Barth makes no such distinction. "[T]he visible and the invisible Church are not two Churches—an earthly-historical fellowship and above and behind this a supra-naturally spiritual fellowship. . . . The mystery is hidden in the form, but represented and to be sought out in it."[5] In Barth's ecclesiology, what happens now in the church is of great importance, and every community must commit to being the true church, acknowledging that we will always be an imperfect and flawed representation of Jesus Christ. Yet this is the work to which we are called as Christians; there is no heavenly vision of a better church in the sweet by-and-by. Because the church is one, Barth has no time for divisions and infighting. Such arguments are not the work of the Holy Spirit but of our own perverse impulses, and they demonstrate a lack of humility and obedience to the Word of God.

Church Dogmatics was written more than fifty years ago, and in that time there has been no end to the fracturing of the Christian community. Even within churches there are often conflicts and divisiveness, sometimes over the most trivial issues. Grounded in Barth's ecclesiology, a pastor can call the community back together and encourage all sides to seek unity through obedience to God.

To understand Barth's view on church unity, it is helpful for me to look at the polity of my tradition, the United Church of Christ. Each congregation is organized as a separate, independent community, with Jesus Christ as the head of every congregation. We are in faithful covenant with all other UCC congregations and with every level of governance within the church, meaning we do not control one another but promise to be guided by obedience to the Spirit and careful attention to what is revealed in Scripture. We say we are a united and uniting church, recognizing that Christian unity is the primary goal of our faith but a goal that can never be reached in this world.

As a UCC pastor, I can tell you that we often lose sight of this core belief, forgetting that it is Jesus who is the head of the church and Jesus who unites us. There are times when petty disagreements or doctrinal differences get out of hand. No one likes conflict—especially in the church—and in my experience, people sometimes avoid dealing with issues directly, mistaking a lack of open conflict for true Christian unity. But according to Barth's theology, if we allow ourselves to be divided and divisive, we cease to be the church. That is how important it is to remain one in Christ. I'm not sure I would ever use such language directly with my congregation, but Barth's theological emphasis on the unity of the church is a sharp reminder of what is at stake when we encounter conflict in a congregation.

Before moving on to the second mark of the church, I want to note that Barth takes a strong stand against individual, private faith. For Barth a person cannot be Christian without being part of a particular church. His argument goes like this: In this time between Easter and the second coming, Jesus is at work in the world as the church, the body of Christ. To be Christian is to be part of the body, and there is no body apart from the church. Now, there are plenty of people who define themselves as Christian, but they find the church to be a failed institution, full of hypocrisy and judgment. Barth acknowledges that the church is a frail institution. Yet to be apart from the church "is to abandon not only the distress but the hope of the community and indeed oneself. For there are no retreats and towers of this kind. We are either in the *communion sanctorum* or we are not *sancti*. A private monadic faith is not the Christian faith."[6] This is a helpful theological argument in a world awash in people who are spiritual but not religious. Of course, Barth does not tie salvation to life in the church, but he does claim that for all its flaws, the church is the only place to be Christian.

The Church Is Holy

The second mark of the church is that it is holy. Barth interprets this to mean that the church is called out by God to be distinct from the world. As members of the church, we bring no holiness of our own to this enterprise. The church is holy because the head of the church, Jesus, is holy. Instead, we are fallible, subject to forces within, such as sin and error, and forces without, such as persecution and temptation. This means that Christians can never take for granted the holiness of the church. We must be ever vigilant, never avoiding self-examination or self-correction. Again, Barth's ecclesiology calls for humility within the church. "When has it been the case that men could simply see the good works of Christians and had to glorify the Father which is in heaven (Mt.5:16)? Taking it all in all, the community of Jesus Christ in the world may at times be clothed with every kind of pomp and glory; but what a frail vessel it is, exposed to every kind of assault, and actually assaulted both outwardly and above all inwardly!"[7]

Yet while Barth warns Christians to be vigilant and self-correcting, we ought not to think that our action or inaction makes the church holy. Here he makes a careful and useful distinction. The activity of the church does not make it holy; it is Jesus Christ who makes the church holy. But the activity of the church *is* the holy work of God. As Christians, we are not called to commit random acts of kindness. There is nothing random in our work. What we do is rooted in and grows out of our obedience to God in Jesus Christ.

As a pastor of a liberal congregation, I appreciate Barth's understanding of holiness because it requires that social action be tied to a living engagement with the Christian faith. I've served a number of congregations that are full of well-meaning, hardworking people committed to making the world a better place. They feed the hungry, house the homeless, and comfort the widows and orphans. But sometimes these same people are less interested in paying attention to God or developing a theological framework for social action. When social action becomes disconnected from faith formation or a pulsing sense of discipleship, the church risks becoming what one critic described as "the Rotary Club with sacraments." Understanding Barth's ecclesiology equips pastors to talk about the importance of nurturing faith.

I would also contend that Barth's ecclesiology helps prioritize activity in the church. Action is critical; thus social action, mission work, and ministry are all necessary if we are to be the church. But the first priority for the church is to understand and witness to what God has done: though we deserve God's judgment and punishment, in Jesus Christ, we have been saved. That is the meaning and message of the cross, the engine that defines and drives the activity of every congregation.

One last word about holiness needs to be said. Although Barth calls the Christian community to humility and obedience for the sake of unity and holiness in the church, this does not mean he takes a soft stance on church discipline. Barth recognizes that it is sometimes necessary—even essential—for the corporate body to make judgments and hold individual members accountable for their behavior or beliefs. He even holds out the possibility that some people ought to be expelled from the church.[8] This in no way affects the individual's ultimate salvation—that is a judgment made by God and separate from church polity. But Barth is clear that the church, in striving to be one and holy, must be prepared to remove people from the rolls if necessary. As a pastor in a denomination that has, at times, tried to be all things to all people, I find this to be a powerful word to hear—some people may need to leave and find another faith community if their beliefs and values are antithetical to the mission of a congregation. Sometimes unity and holiness require firm judgment and hard decisions.

The Church Is Catholic

Barth hits his theological stride when he explores the meaning of the third mark of the church: the church is catholic. For Barth, this word has multiple meanings—geographic, temporal, and eternal. And with every nuance of definition, there is a word of wisdom for the church today.

Catholic has a geographic dimension. It means that the church is the same (universal) no matter where it is. In every society, in every time, and in every part of the world, it is the same Spirit who animates the church, the same Christ who is the head. Barth goes further: because the church (generally) is made manifest in particular places among particular people, it is right that church life take many forms—that is, the impulse to "be church" is expressed through different human societies. No one human society has the right to dictate the particular form that church takes. Rather than being appalled by the diversity of the Christian church today, I believe Barth would see it as a mark of catholic authenticity. While this might seem to contradict Barth's views on division in the church, it doesn't. Barth applauds diversity in the expression of the faith, but he abhors division in the understanding of the faith. In other words, there is one faith as there is one Christ, but each church is a unique body, gifted and called to live out the one faith in a multitude of ways.

Yet Barth offers a word of caution on this subject. Every church should be an authentic expression of the body of Christ, but care must be taken so that accommodation to social values and customs does not undermine the gospel. "In all the apparently unavoidable accommodations of a practical and technical kind, [the church] must see to it that it does not become guilty of deviation from the way which can only be the same in all spheres, or of disloyalty to the commission which it has to discharge in them all."[9] I don't think Barth is against incorporating the unique characteristics and forms of human society into the life of the church, but he worries about the tail of society wagging the dog of the church. Vigilance, obedience, and humility are the keys.

I have often wondered about the problem of accommodation and how quickly it can erode the mission of the church. Some church development consultants tout the power of modern technology as a tool for church growth and evangelism. Certainly many congregations have gone "high tech" to great effect. But I've seen worship services where the method overtakes the message. After attending a contemporary worship service complete with a rock band in a big evangelical worship center, I heard one young man say to another, "That was great! I hardly knew I was in church at all!" Barth's advice is to be mindful of how you cater to the changeable tastes of society lest you win the battle but lose the war.

Catholic, understood as a temporal category, means something else to Barth. Seen through this lens, the catholic church is the church of the present moment, called to evangelize. Everyone is called into the church. This is a gospel demand to evangelize not just those people who are like us or who meet some suspect test for saintliness. This is the open door, the wide net, the welcome embrace of Christ. This evangelical imperative pinches liberal and conservative churches alike. Speaking from a liberal perspective, we are not big on evangelizing. In fact, the word makes us uncomfortable. We respect diversity and freedom and believe that everyone should be able to make their own choices without us imposing our own beliefs. But how can people make a decision if they lack information? As Paul writes in Romans, "For, 'Everyone who calls on the name of the Lord shall be saved.' But how are they to call on one in whom they have not believed? And how are they to believe in one of whom they have never heard? And how are they to hear without someone to proclaim him? And how are they to proclaim him unless they are sent? As it is written, 'How beautiful are the feet of those who bring good news!'" (Rom. 10:13-15). If the church is to be the church, it must evangelize, even if it makes us nervous.

For more conservative Christians, the universal call of the church challenges the tendency of some congregations to preclude certain people from membership. If the church is one holy, catholic church, there can be no "presorting" of people. We are all equally and simultaneously saints and sinners; if anyone is welcome, all are welcome. Yet there are some Christian communities who fear being corrupted by certain kinds of people, avoiding any association with them whatsoever. Case in point: Our church recently purchased a new copier and found ourselves with an extra Xerox machine.

The Xerox representative put us in touch with a small inner-city church, and we called to see if they wanted the old copier. Initially they expressed interest, but when they found out we are an open and affirming congregation (i.e., one that welcomes gays and lesbians into full Christian fellowship), they declined the offer. Why? Because they didn't want their ministry to be tainted by our false doctrine. If the church is to be the church, I think Barth would counsel erring on the side of inclusion.

There is one final way to understand *catholic* as Barth sees it, and that is as an eternal body. Barth explains that every church is part of the eternal church, that timeless communion of saints. As such, the highest priority for any church is to remain truthful to the gospel of Jesus Christ. This requires faith. (In fact, Barth believes that every mark of the church requires faith to evaluate whether a particular community is living out the call to be the one holy, catholic, apostolic church.) It is also no guarantee of success; in fact, sometimes maintaining the truth of the gospel sets the church at odds with society. In other words, don't be misled by success. "Certainly great membership rolls and good attendance and full churches and lecture halls are facts which naturally impress us—who can fail to be impressed by them?—but what do they really have to do with the truth?"[10] In Barth's ecclesiology any church that holds to the truth, continually seeking God's will in humble obedience, is a success.

This definition of *catholic* is good news for churches, especially the many small and struggling congregations that feel defeated by declining enrollment and lack of resources. In a world where the success of megachurches is studied and glorified, it is a relief to hear someone say that any Christian community that holds to the truth has succeeded. Furthermore, Barth's demand for the truth to be preached in every church, in every season, puts a little steel in this preacher's spine. As a pastor, if I see my church through the lens of Barth's ecclesiology, I am not just given permission to preach on difficult issues—I am required to do so for the sake of the congregation.

The Church Is Apostolic

From Barth's distinctly Protestant perspective, the apostolic nature of the church is a spiritual criterion rather than a historical or juridical one. "Apostolic means in the discipleship, in the school, under the normative authority, instruction and direction of the apostles."[11] Barth takes a moment to dismiss the idea of apostolic succession as a valid criterion for identifying the true church, not because it strains credibility to suggest that there is an unbroken line of bishops tracing back to the apostles, but because such a criterion is divorced from faith, devoid of the Holy Spirit. "It is obvious that neither the Holy Spirit nor faith is necessary for this purpose, but only an uncritical or critical archeological knowledge of the lists."[12]

Having established apostolicity as a spiritual criterion, Barth explores how the apostolic nature of the church interacts with the other three marks. One way to think of it as the last mark is as the teacher of the others. In other words, an apostolic church is one that is obedient to the teachings of Scripture and relies on the wisdom of the apostles as part of the ongoing self-examination and correction necessary for remaining one, holy, and catholic. This might strike the reader as obvious, but frankly it is nice for the pastor of a liberal congregation to have an ecclesiological justification for Bible study.

Beyond the Nicene Creed

Barth's ecclesiology goes beyond the four marks of the church. For one thing, he makes clear that the church, either as a body of believers or as an institution, should not be worshipped. No church, even a good church, is worthy of worship. This poses a challenge to those of us who serve large, institutional congregations. Having just completed a $2.2 million renovation project, I'm sensitive to Barth's critique, aware that large edifices make tempting idols. Having clarity about the theological purpose of the church helps me balance the need to have a facility that supports ministry against the desire to have an impressive building.

For Barth the church is always on the move, traveling by the Holy Spirit between the resurrection and the second coming, the consummation of God's activity in the world. Because of this, there is no golden age. It is always ahead of us. Yet how many churches look longingly back at the 1950s, when the pews were full and preachers were the arbiters of moral judgment? Such spiritual nostalgia can suck the life out of a congregation, giving members the impression that the best times are behind them. But that's not true. Until the return of Jesus, the best is yet to come. This ecclesiology gives every church a reason to pull for the far horizon.

Throughout Barth's ecclesiology, he calls the church to live in humility, obedience, and faith. These virtues are in short supply, particularly in American society. Some people do not even consider these to be virtues. And this is not all the church is called to do in the world. There are times the church must be prophetic, compassionate, demanding, meditative, protective, or celebratory. The church needs to take risks for the sake of the gospel, even in the full knowledge that we will undoubtedly make mistakes. But every moment in the life of a true church must be rooted in those original virtues: humility, obedience, and faith. This is the only way, according to Barth, we can hope to be the real church, the body of Christ in the world.

One final aspect of Barth's ecclesiology that I find fascinating is his sure belief that the church is the place where the Spirit is at work. I don't altogether subscribe to this point of view, for I believe there is such a thing as general revelation. But for Barth the church is the only place for true communion with the Spirit; if you want to be Christian, you need to show up in church. As I mentioned above, it's not a matter of salvation, but for those who have been baptized into the Christian faith, life in the church is the work to which we have been called. This is the way of life.

Toward the end of his discussion of ecclesiology, Barth wonders why there is a church. "Would it not have better served both the glory of God and the salvation of man if all that has happened since [the resurrection] had not happened, if that eternal Sabbath had in fact begun?"[13] Barth does not answer this question, only marvels at the meaning of this mystery. "But that is how it is. And if that is how it is, it is obvious that He still has a goal and goals, that He still expects something in the world and humanity created and preserved by Him. He has spoken His final Word, but He has not yet finished speaking it."[14] In this midst of this marvelous time, moving from the first parousia to the second, how exciting it is to be the form of God's ongoing work in the world!

Coda: The Meaning of Silver

What at first seemed like a petty dispute over the use of the silver service revealed a deep division in my congregation that cut along generational lines. Resolving this dispute required more than an opinion on the subject of platters and teapots; it required seeing the conflict through the lens of ecclesiology.

When pressed to explain why using the silver service was important, one matriarch said, "These aren't just pieces of silver. They were given by people who lived lives of service. Giving up the silver is like forgetting them and forgetting who we are. It's part of our history." She had a catholic understanding of the church, seeing it as a community that exists as part of an ongoing history that shapes the church's identity and activity. In her mind the silver was a spiritual asset, imbued with moral value.

One of the younger women stopped by my office later that day. She had given some thought to her "anti-silver" stance and wanted to clarify her position. "I know the silver is important to some people, but we simply don't have the extra time it would take to polish the service before the event, to say nothing of cleaning it up afterward. I feel like the older women think I'm lazy. But I'm not lazy; I'm busy." She understood the church as a place of God's activity here and now. In the midst of her busy life, she was willing to be part of this body of Christ, but she didn't see any inherent Christian value in the fancy serving ware. We agreed to meet one more time to try to resolve the issue.

At the next planning meeting, I opened the conversation with a reflection on what it means to be the church. I praised the church for its faithful service to the community and for the remarkable hospitality for which we are known. Then I said, "But Christian service is more than something we do for outsiders. We are also called to serve one another in a spirit of love. In a spirit of love, sometimes we make special accommodations or honor the opinions of others. In a spirit of love, sometimes we do a little more so everyone can participate in the mission and work of this church. Whatever we do, we are one body, and our first impulse should be to serve God by building each other up." There was a moment of quiet.

"We could use the silver," said the chair of the planning committee. "But we'll need some help getting it ready." "We'll take care of the silver," said the president of the Women's Fellowship. "You don't have to worry about it."

This is the church at its best, one holy, catholic, and apostolic body of Christ, where the common ground is holy ground.

The Empty Church
Shannon Craigo-Snell

Sunday Morning

My kids wake me up at the crack of dawn on Sunday, just like every other day. This is followed by a rare moment of peace and calm in my otherwise hectic week. The children watch cartoons in the living room while I—wonder of wonders—drink coffee and read the *New York Times* at the kitchen table.

It doesn't last long. Within fifteen or twenty minutes, the boys are eager for breakfast and making plans for the rest of the day. Those moments at the table, communing with my coffee and paper, are lovely. Every other morning is a race to get things done and get out of the house—so why in the world would I hurry breakfast and hustle the kids to get to church on Sunday? While I deeply appreciate Barth's theology, especially in Shawnthea's lucid prose, "one, holy, catholic, and apostolic" simply cannot compete with the possibility of Sabbath at home. One, holy, catholic, and apostolic will not get me out of bed on Sunday morning.

Plus there is a risk. If I decide to leave the coffee and the paper and go to church, what will I get in exchange for my time? My theological standards are high. Will the preacher offer theological reflections that pass muster? Will the service give adequate attention to the diversity of the Christian tradition and the nuances of biblical hermeneutics? Shawnthea notes that some people get nervous when evangelism is mentioned. I don't get nervous; I break out in hives.

So what are my options? Do I abandon the church and focus solely on theology? I confess I am tempted, but Shawnthea has convinced me that this is not a workable option. When I begin to separate Christian theology from the church, she pulls me back every time. What I need, then, is a new account of Christian church that can speak to me today, one that can reinvigorate this doctrine and address my current situation.

Constructive Theology

In chapter 2, I described a discipline within the field of theology called systematic theology. Close kin to systematics is a discipline called constructive theology. In this arena, theologians offer their own creative insights on theological issues, topics, doctrines, or debates. Constructive theology is not in contrast to systematic theology. Many systematic theologians are also constructive theologians and vice versa. Nevertheless, it is possible to engage in one discipline without the other.

Within Christianity, constructive theology happens in conversation with traditional views. This means that a constructive theologian does not start from scratch or simply make things up according to her own desires. Instead, she looks closely at the accumulated wisdom of Christian writers and communities over the years and brings this wisdom into dialogue with contemporary situations. Constructive theological proposals are particularly useful when traditional formulations of doctrines or issues lose some of their strength. This happens often and for many reasons. Sometimes words once crucial to articulating an idea can become unfamiliar and therefore less useful, such as *hypostatic union* or *transubstantiation*. Sometimes history unfolds in ways that expose Christian formulations as complicit with oppression. For example, after World War II, Christians had to rethink any theological claims that could foster anti-Semitism and that may have contributed to genocide. Similarly, heightened awareness of sexism and racism demands that theologians reexamine theological positions or assumptions that undergird prejudice, fear, and hate. Sometimes the metaphors that once gave life to theological claims simply become less invigorating. Calvin's description of sin as an infection probably seemed direr before the age of antibiotics, though perhaps to return to new strength in light of the AIDS epidemic. For many different reasons, the vibrancy of Christian theology depends on the new proposals, imaginative recastings, and constructive insights of contemporary theologians.

One of the exciting characteristics of constructive theology is that it often involves creative engagement with other academic disciplines. Constructive theologians draw on the ideas and insights of other fields of knowledge in order to think more fully and more creatively about particularly theological questions. One of the primary conversation partners for theology over the centuries has been philosophy. In the modern era, history has been a valuable interlocutor. Now theologians engage the work of sociologists, theorists, economists, physicists, and myriad others.

I think ecclesiology (the doctrine of the church) is ripe for constructive reconfiguration. Given that many communities in Europe and the United States have found their churches growing emptier as the twenty-first century progresses, perhaps I am not alone in succumbing to the allure of coffee and newspaper. It's time to rethink what it means to be the church.

Performing the Church

I want to begin this work by changing the focus, asking not what it means to *be* church, but what it is to *do* church. Church is not just something we think about; it is something we do. Christianity is not a series of intellectual propositions that we believe. Rather, it is a way of living in the world that shapes and is shaped by our embodied and communal lives. This is seen nowhere more clearly than in the church when we gather together to perform actions that are deeply related to what we believe but certainly more than just a recital of preconceived ideas. Our participation in the activity of church is a profound reminder that Christianity is not a philosophy or an intellectual system of disembodied knowledge. It is a way of acting and being in the world; it is something we perform. For this reason, I find the most helpful partners in conversation on ecclesiology to be performance studies and theatre studies.

The field of performance studies has been developing in the past thirty years, with roots in many disciplines, including linguistics, sociology, and anthropology.[15] Given the diversity of scholars who are interested in performance, it is not surprising that there is a lot of debate about what performance actually is. For my purposes here, I want to sketch three characteristics that are common to many different types of performance.[16] First, performance is an event. It is not a static entity but something that takes place in a particular time and context. Second, performance involves interaction. It is easiest to think of this in terms of actors and audience, although the idea can be more broadly understood. Finally, performance involves a peculiar kind of doubleness, in which there is a gap between what someone does and an ideal, model, or remembered version of that same action.[17] For example, imagine an actor performing *King Lear*. The actor has a vision of *Lear* in his head, constructed from the script and his own thoughts about it and from a version he saw on PBS as a child. Even though he attempts to fully embody this ideal on the stage, he is never going to completely *be* King Lear; there will always be a gap, a doubleness between the actor and the character.

Performance studies is not primarily concerned with deciding what *is* and *is not* a performance. Instead, it is a way of looking at various activities *as* performances, employing a particular analytic framework.[18] Given the three general characteristics of performance I have highlighted, to look at something *as* a performance is to pay attention to the way in which it is an action, involves interaction, and includes doubleness. This substantially broadens the scope of performance. As event, performance would include not only the production of a play or the singing of a song. It could also include the reading of a book.[19] The book itself is not a performance, but every time someone picks it up and reads it, that event can be interpreted as a performance.

Similarly, the idea of interaction is broadened. A painting on a wall in an unoccupied room is hard to understand as a performance, but the moment a person views the painting, that event can be seen as a performance, involving multiple interactions. There is an interaction between a painter who worked a hundred years ago, the culture that he lived in that shaped his art, a contemporary viewer who sees the painting today, and the current culture that has been influenced by this painting and also influences how the viewer interprets it. Note that because a performance is an event, the context (time, place, culture, etc.) in which it takes place always plays a role in the interaction.[20] Finally, the doubleness that I described above applies not only to an actor playing Lear, but also to an athlete striving to be a faster, stronger version of herself, as well as to a newly married woman who cleans the house and makes dinner in an effort to fill the role of daughter-in-law.[21]

I find the concept of performance to be helpful in thinking about ecclesiology because it draws attention to some of the most basic properties of what church is: it is an event and it involves interaction. As straightforward as this is as an observation, these characteristics of church often do not figure prominently in discussions about the nature, purpose, and meaning of church. I also think the property of doubleness is prominent in church. In liturgy and ritual, we repeat actions we have models of in our minds and memories as we attempt to live into a future we have not yet fully seen. Performance studies, then, can help frame an analysis of church that draws these characteristics—event, interaction, and doubleness—into focus. Because these characteristics are so vital to church and so easily overlooked in the process of reading and writing about the church, I think performance studies is a valuable dialogue partner for constructive ecclesiology.

Theatre and Church

I want to engage theatre studies, particularly, because it holds abundant and rich resources for discussing how meaning is conveyed and created in embodied, communal performances. One such resource so quickly resonates with ideas about the church that it serves as a smooth entryway into this interdisciplinary discussion.[22] In the book *The Empty Space,* director Peter Brook offers an analysis of four types of theatre as both a diagnosis of what has gone wrong in the theatre and a vision of hope for what can go right. His descriptions are about theatre, yet they are also recognizable as descriptions of churches that might be encountered across America. Brook begins by noting the ambiguity of the term *theatre.* He writes:

> I can take any empty space and call it a bare stage. A man walks across this empty space and whilst someone else is watching him, and this is all that is needed for an act of theatre to be engaged. Yet when we talk about theatre this is not quite what we mean. Red curtains, spotlights, blank verse, laughter, darkness, these are all confusedly superimposed in a messy image covered by one all-purpose word.[23]

Already some similarities with the word *church* appear. Church, like theatre, can happen in any empty space. A Pentecostal friend of mine sometimes says, "We had church." She might be referring to a deeply successful worship service or a phone call with a friend, as she uses the word *church* to describe something that happened rather than a particular setting or group of people. Also like *theatre*, the word *church* is used in many different ways. It can refer to the church building, to the congregation, or to events that happen within the church building among the congregation.

Brook does not immediately parse the word *theatre* into a precise definition. Instead, he describes four types of theatre that are often mixed together. Over the course of discussing these four types—Deadly, Holy, Rough, and Immediate—Brook points the reader to an understanding of theatre that is less a precise definition than a shared vision of possible beauty. Brook's typology therefore serves less as a system of classification than as a call to aspiration. Following his pattern of thought about theatre can be illuminating for understanding, transforming, and performing church.

Deadly

The first type of theatre Brook addresses is the Deadly. This one is easily recognizable because it is bad. One of the major causes of Deadly Theatre is when tradition becomes more important than current meaning. Imagine a production of one of Shakespeare's plays, where the actors appear in resplendent period costume, speak in noble and elevated tones, and deliver to the audience exactly what is expected of Shakespearean drama. This, Brook says, is deadly.

> The Deadly Theatre takes easily to Shakespeare. We see his plays done by good actors in what seems like the proper way—they look lively and colourful, there is music and everyone is all dressed up, just as they are supposed to be in the best of classical theatres. Yet secretly we find it excruciatingly boring—and in our hearts we either blame Shakespeare, or theatre as such, or even ourselves.[24]

The Deadly Theatre is supported and continued by deadly critics (who may love the theatre or have grown to hate it, but either way have no clearly articulated vision of what it might be),[25] deadly actors (concerned more for their image than their craft),[26] and even deadly spectators. Deadly spectators go to the theatre because it is expected of people in their cultural set, or because their spouses insist.[27] They arrive with clear expectations of what good theatre looks like and are complacently content when nothing about the production departs from the form in their minds, when nothing is too intense or too distracting.

For me, Brook's description of Deadly Theatre immediately conjures images of particular churches I have known. Beautiful churches that look exactly like churches are supposed to, where there is the reassuring comfort of knowing what to expect, where any given Sunday might bring a new insight to ponder but will not upset the applecart of my own understanding of Christianity. Nothing is too intense or too distracting. These churches are filled with people who come to church on Sunday because it is good for their children, or it provides a moral background for middle-class family life, or it is expected of people in their family or community.

While Brook's diagnosis of this problem in the theatre might be helpful for recognizing problems in the church, his analysis of the cause is disturbing. Although there are many contributing factors to deadliness, tradition is a leading cause. Repeating something over and over again—from a particular production to a general way of approaching Shakespeare—kills the vitality of theatre. He writes, "Theatre is always a self-destructive art, and it is always written on the wind. A professional theatre assembles different people every night and speaks to them through the language of behaviour. A performance gets set and usually has to be repeated—and repeated as well and accurately as possible—but from the day it is set something invisible is beginning to die."[28]

It might seem that Brook's comments could not be useful to understanding the church since Christian worship embraces tradition, ritual, and repetition as vital elements. Yet Brook says that tradition does not have to be deadly. It is possible to pass knowledge and ritual from one generation to the next in such a way that "meaning . . . that is communicated—and meaning never belongs to the past."[29] In other words, tradition becomes deadly when it is not the meaning that is passed on, but the trappings. Precisely in attempting to focus on eternal truths (say, for instance, in a Shakespearean play), theatre companies attempt to avoid "superficial variations" that reflect the current culture, relying instead on conceptions of noble and larger-than-life ways of communicating.[30] This produces the opposite of its intended effect; the abiding meaning is lost as the repetition of old forms takes precedence.

Whenever churches hold on to traditional ways of doing things simply because they are traditional, we are moving toward deadly church. Theologian Letty Russell spoke of the "Strawberry Festival Syndrome." Many churches in Connecticut have strawberry festivals in the spring when the weather finally breaks and the berries are ripe. Russell said that if you ask people in these churches why they have strawberry festivals, many say, "Because we always have had one." That kind of tradition, divorced from communication or the creation of meaning in the present, is what Brook identifies as deadly in the theatre, and I think it is deadly in the church. Ritual and tradition can be amazing ways to generate, communicate, and facilitate communal meaning in church, but when we repeat for the sake of repetition, then the church moves toward the kind of respectable, slightly boring, cultural establishment that the Deadly Theatre has become.

Holy

Next Brook describes the Holy Theatre, or the "Theatre of the Invisible-Made-Visible."[31] Here Brook is knee-deep in the tricky business of describing and defining something ineffable. To conjure the vision of theatre he wants to communicate, Brook falls back on language of religion and magic and on the assumption that his readers already know what it looks like. He writes of rituals and orphic rites, of possession, incarnation, and even the cross. Brook says that many people "have seen the face of the invisible through an experience on the stage that transcended their experience in life."[32] He tries to evoke a memory of when theatre has been holy by describing particular scenes in which something holy took place. One of the most potent among these vignettes is the account of poor children in Hamburg in 1946. Brook writes:

> I saw a crowd of children pushing excitedly into a night club door. I followed them. On the stage was a bright blue sky. Two seedy, spangled clowns sat on a painted cloud on their way to visit the Queen of Heaven. "What shall we ask her for?" said one. "Dinner," said the other, and the children screamed approval. "What shall we have for dinner?" "Schinken, leberwurst . . ." The clown began to list all the unobtainable foods, and the squeals of excitement were gradually replaced by a hush—a hush that settled into a deep and true theatrical silence. An image was being made real, in answer to the need for something that was not there.[33]

With this story, Brook points toward the holy, toward moments when the audience sees something happen onstage that is more and other than—but never removed from—this world as we know it day to day.

When it comes to a straightforward definition, Brook claims Holy Theatre makes visible the invisible, and it responds to a hunger.

It is not just any hunger. Holy Theatre responds to "a hunger for the invisible, a hunger for reality deeper than the fullest form of everyday life." It is not merely the fulfillment of a "hunger for the missing things of life, [but] a hunger, in fact, for buffers against reality."[34] Furthermore, "Holy [T]heatre not only presents the invisible but also offers conditions that make its perception possible."[35]

Throughout his description of Holy Theatre, Brook offers some suggestions for moving toward it. We should not be afraid of silence.[36] We should recognize that ritual is something we desperately need and that it can be supersaturated with meaning in ways that narration cannot.[37] While we should be careful of tradition for tradition's sake, if we attempt to find the holy outside of any tradition, we can end up with "a rich but dangerous eclecticism," one that attempts to gain the holy through addition when subtraction is a better path.[38]

Each of these ideas resonates with my own experiences of church communities attempting to see the invisible, to encounter the holy. My favorite line from Brook's discussion of Holy Theatre stands as a condemnation of much of the complacent culture of American Christianity, in which we have so often not seen the holy that we stop expecting the invisible to appear and instead accept that Sunday mornings in church help hold our families together, teach our children ethics, and provide us with a community of like-minded people in our town. Brook writes, "It is not the fault of the holy that it has become a middle-class weapon to keep children good."[39]

Brook's description of Holy Theatre is far from a systematic theological treatise. It is a gesture toward something that does not happen often, but which Brook himself is sure is possible. He holds on to memories of the moments when the invisible was visible, and by narrating them he challenges readers to remember the occasions when they have seen it too.

Rough

After scaling the heights of the Holy Theatre, Brook moves on to the popular theatre, for it "saves the day."[40] This is theatre that can happen anywhere, and indeed most often comes to be outside conventional theatre buildings. It is bawdy and raucous, disorderly and loud. Brook writes, "It is most of all dirt that gives the roughness its edge; filth and vulgarity are natural, obscenity is joyous; with these the spectacle takes on its socially liberating role, for by nature the popular theatre is anti-authoritarian, anti-traditional, anti-pomp, anti-pretence."[41]

Brook contrasts the Holy and Rough Theatres, saying that they are antagonistic to one another. "If the [H]oly makes a world in which a prayer is more real than a belch, in the [R]ough [T]heatre, it is the other way round. The belching then is real and prayer would be considered comic."[42] He continues, "The Holy Theatre has one energy, the Rough has others. Lightheartedness and gaiety feeds it, but so does the same energy that produces rebellion and opposition. This is a militant energy: it is the energy of anger, sometimes the energy of hate."[43]

It might be hard to imagine how such a theatre is cast as saving the day for Brook, and even harder to imagine how it could be connected to the church. For Brook the Rough Theatre is vital because it upsets the Deadly Theatre and brings theatre back into the role of satisfying hunger. Rough Theatre is profoundly connected to the messy realities of life; it celebrates them, laughs at them, tells the truth about them, and sometimes aims to change them.

Brook's image of the Rough Theatre is vulgar and bawdy. When I look for a parallel to Rough Theatre in the church, I think of children. There are many churches in which children are not even seen, much less heard. Yet there are also rough churches, where the children, with all their messiness, sticky fingers, runny noses, noise, and unpredictability, are part and parcel of the congregation.

In a rough church, the kids run around the minute the service is over with a freedom and authority that declare the building is their rightful domain and they belong.

In the same way that the Rough Theatre pushes against the Deadly, so too the welcomed presence of children in church moves against deadliness and connects the congregation to the messy realities of life. One Sunday morning my youngest was just old enough to be learning how to manage the difficulties of snaps, buttons, and zippers. He had dressed himself in an outfit of clashing colors that he wore with pride. During the children's sermon, he went to the front of the church with all the other children and sat down on the floor. A few minutes later, I noticed that he was fussing with the buttons of his shirt. Wedged in the middle of a pew, several rows back, I watched as my dear child began to undress himself, step by step, in front of the altar. In a deadly church, his actions would have been cause for great embarrassment. In this church, however, they were met with happy laughter, while another mother, sitting in a front pew, got down on the floor to help my son get dressed again. Of course this G-rated event is not what Brook describes as Rough Theatre, but I think the same elements of real life—sweat, noise, and smell—are all here, acting as a corrective to pretense and pomp.

Rough Theatre and church also connect when it comes to social action. Telling the truth about real life is often the first and necessary step toward changing unjust social conditions. The Rough Theatre, with the energy of rebellion and revolution, poses the questions "What is our purpose, now, in relation to people we meet every day? Do we need liberation? From what? In what way?"[44] These are the same questions churches should be asking, and many do. Wrestling with harsh realities—from the joy and exhaustion of parenting to the despair and anger of injustice—is part of what the church is called to do.

Although the Holy and Rough Theatres are irreconcilable, Brook holds up the combination of the two as his ideal of what theatre ought to be.[45] He is aiming for the holy, for the invisible-made-visible. He wants theatre to respond to the need for a reality deeper than the everyday. He writes, "We need desperately to experience magic in so direct a way that our very notion of what is substantial could be changed."[46] That is Holy Theatre, but we cannot get there by aiming for the holy alone. Attempts at pure holiness are deadly, for they step away from the rough realities of life. Brook's model, of course, is Shakespeare. Brook writes of the bard:

> His aim continually is holy, metaphysical, yet he never makes the mistake of staying too long on the highest plane. He knew how hard it is for us to keep company with the absolute—so he continually bumps us down to earth. . . . We have to accept that we can never see all of the invisible. So after straining towards it, we have to face defeat, drop down to earth, then start up again.[47]

It is here, in his description of holy and rough together, unreconciled and yet speaking a larger truth in their connection, that I find Brook most theologically compelling. He is speaking about incarnation—the meeting of divinity and humanity. The two are unmixed and inseparable, truly together yet not the same. Brook says that when we encounter this, we can respond with our whole selves—emotionally and intellectually, subjectively and politically.[48] And he warns us that sometimes in our desire for the holy, we look for the trappings of nobility and find only the deadly, when the holy is much more likely to be found in the noise and smells of the rough.

Immediate

If that Holy-Rough Theatre of Shakespeare satisfies the hunger for a deeper reality, for magic that changes our sense of what is substantial, then Immediate Theatre tries to "evoke in audiences an undeniable hunger and thirst."[49] Brook is aiming for that incarnational mixture of Holy and Rough, and he describes his own efforts as Immediate Theatre. He summarizes his reflections on his work by drawing on English translations of three French words used to describe the theatre: *repetition, representation,* and *assistance.*[50] Repetition evokes both the sense of discipline and effort that goes into creating theatre, and the danger of deadliness. Good theatre requires the skills and abilities that can come about only through nearly endless repetition. Yet the very repetition that enables meaning-making in the theatre always threatens to destroy it, to make it into concretized tradition that holds meaning no longer.[51] Representation is the way out of the trap of repetition, for representation constantly "makes present," denying time by making meanings of the past immediate again.[52] Finally, in French one of the words for a spectator in an audience means one who assists.[53] Assistance is rendered by the audience to the theatre company, "and at the same time for the audience itself assistance comes back from the stage."[54] For Brook the best theatre happens when the lines between audience and actor blur. The artist can challenge the audience best when "he is a spike in the side of an audience that is determined to challenge itself. He celebrates with an audience most truly when he is the mouthpiece of an audience that has a ground of joy."[55]

In this final discussion, Brook sounds to me like a minister who is both ambitious and humble, trying hard to create a space in which something magic—something he believes is truly possible—can happen. He does not take credit for such magic happening. That is beyond what he can do. But he can attempt to generate the hunger and thirst for that magic, for the invisible-made-visible, for the incarnational meeting of human and divine. In speaking of his own theatrical methods, Brook writes nothing in stone. Every tactic is provisional; a whole barrage of possibilities can and must be used in response to the particular situation that arises. This reminds me of watching Shawnthea at work. For a pastor, the goal of ministry is more important than the kinds of methodological purity that we value in academia. And there is always a humility that comes from a deep love of the theatre, or the church, and which is ultimately rooted in faith in the magic that is sometimes experienced there.

Analogy and Insight

The process of looking at ecclesiology and Brook's work on theatre side by side is an approach based on analogy and aims to uncover new insights. Understanding theatre as performance (as event, interaction, and doubleness) highlights ways in which theatre and church, although very different, are also analogous. Thus Brook's thoughtful comments about theatre can be mined for insights that might be of use to ecclesiology.

Here is some of what I find useful in his work. First, tradition can be deadly if it is divorced from communal meaning-making in the present. Second, in church as in theatre, there are times when the invisible is made visible and when a real hunger is met. When this happens, we can experience something that changes our perceptions and expectations about what is possible in the world. Third, striving for the holy must always be held in tension with the rough and messy realities of everyday life. Fourth, to foster the hunger that is met by the incarnational meeting of holy and rough, we have the immediate, which is created by a communal commitment to repetition, representation, and assistance. Such insights are the beginning of a constructive reworking of ecclesiology that has the potential to get me to the church on time.

Revisiting Sundays

I said above that one, holy, catholic, and apostolic are not enough to get me moving on Sunday mornings. It's true. But when I look at the church through Brook's eyes, I am reminded that I have seen the invisible there; I have encountered the holy. The rough realities of life are acknowledged there, as my children run wild and the pastor speaks about growing homelessness in New Haven. Something powerful does not always happen in church on Sunday mornings, but sometimes it does. I do not know any way to make it happen every Sunday, because it is ultimately dependent on the Spirit of God instead of human action. But I do know that we can help to create a space in which it is possible that the invisible might be made visible, and might even be perceived as such. Creating such a space will involve the sometimes difficult discipline of repetition—going every Sunday until the words of the hymns are written on my tongue and the biblical characters are familiar friends to my children. It will include representation, as we communally reenact and perform the Christian stories and rituals that make meaning from the past present today. And it will include assistance, for we all are responsible for doing the things that help make the church a space where holiness happens. Suddenly coffee and the *New York Times* seem less compelling.

Coda

I have no desire to create an entire ecclesiology out of Peter Brook's *The Empty Space.* He is not talking about the church in this text, and he never mentions Jesus. But I find him a fascinating conversation partner. If I were to use Brook as a resource in developing a full-blown ecclesiology, the next thing I might do is put him in direct conversation with traditional ecclesiologies. My first choice would be the work of Karl Barth, and what makes me think pairing Barth and Brook might be rewarding is the simple idea of emptiness.

Christians get nervous when churches get empty, when attendance is down and the spaces in the pews seem larger and larger. There has been a lot of talk about whether and why mainline Protestant churches in America and Europe have declining memberships. Academics struggle to find the causes and the cure, while dwindling congregations struggle to keep the lights on and the doors open in buildings too big for their numbers.[56] The idea of an empty church is frightening to many Christians.

In contrast, Brook frames his entire discussion of the theatre with the idea that theatre can happen in any empty space. An empty space, a person to walk across it, another to be an audience, and theatre can happen. Theatre is a performance. It is an event, an interaction, a doubleness.

While many contemporary Christians get nervous about empty churches, Barth talks about church in terms that resonate with Brook and with the concept of performance. Barth speaks about church as an event, explores the interactions that take place in it, and even, in different words, describes a sort of doubleness. The main event was the act of God in Jesus. Our actions and interactions as communities of Christians are grateful responses to that act of God that we remember in Jesus and look forward to in the parousia. And Barth describes church as empty. The terms he uses for this are steeped in the imagery of war, as he, like Brook, wrote with vivid memories of war-torn Europe. In between World War I and World War II, Barth wrote, "The activity of the [Christian] community is related to the Gospel only in so far as it is no more than a crater formed by the explosion of a shell and seeks to be no more than a void in which the Gospel reveals itself."[57] Barth envisions church as a bombed-out crater, a void left by the penetrating, shattering event of Jesus Christ. He honors the emptiness of this crater and warns against trying to fill it up with our own religious content. In that case "content would be substituted for a void, convex for concave, positive for negative, and the characteristic marks of Christianity would be possession and self-sufficiency rather than deprivation and hope."[58]

Well before he described church in the traditional terms of one, holy, catholic, and apostolic, the young Barth declared that the church was an empty space left by the event of Jesus and demanded that this space be left empty. He did not write in Brook's terms of hunger and magic, but rather in theological terms of deprivation and hope. Brook and Barth are very different authors, in different fields, with different commitments. Yet both men honor an empty space in which, sometimes, the holy is revealed.

Five

Heaven

Shannon: I vividly remember sitting on a town green in Connecticut watching fireworks on the Fourth of July, shamelessly eavesdropping on the family behind me. I was in graduate school, studying the nuances of Christian doctrine and complex issues in contemporary social theory. I had worked all day, until my husband convinced me to take a break and go see the fireworks. As we delighted in the shimmering colors, a little girl behind us posed a theological question: "Can Grandma see the fireworks from heaven?" I listened as her mother and aunt took the girl's question very seriously and began a sincere and thoughtful conversation surrounding it. I was amazed by the enormous difference between the questions asked in my classes and the question asked by these Christians on a summer evening.

One of the characteristics of Christian faith is hope. We have hope for the future, hope for the coming of the new creation, hope for life after death. Our hope is for individuals, for the whole human community, and for the entire cosmos. Christian hope is a vital aspect of the doctrine of eschatology, or last things. Here we do not offer a comprehensive eschatology, but rather we pick up on one particular strand of Christian hope, the hope that individual persons will be held in existence in communion with God after death. When stripped of all the imagery of clouds and pearly gates, this is the hope for heaven. Our approach to this topic is to engage the particular questions of particular Christians.

Theological Restraints

Shannon: In speaking of heaven, theologians are bound on both sides, by the known and the unknown. Given that we do not have a map of heaven from our own experience or from Scripture, we always have to be aware of what we do not know. Also, what knowledge we do have reminds us that the shift from earthly life to heaven is a major transformation. Our hope in heaven is based on the resurrection of Jesus; it is hope that we will be resurrected from death to life eternal. Resurrection is not reanimation. The change that happens in the movement from earthly life to eternal life is not one in which we pick up where we left off before death, even with healed or improved bodies. The coming of the new creation is a culmination of the redemptive grace of God, which is always surprising us, surpassing our wildest hopes of glory. Thus we must remember that when it comes to heaven, we do not know.

On the other side, we are bound by what we do know. We know something of the character of God. We know something of the character of humanity. We know something of how God chooses to relate to humanity in redeeming grace. We also make claims—shifting and conditional as they are—about the nature of creation, the meaning of the resurrection of Jesus, and the continuing work of God in the Holy Spirit. Our attempts to understand heaven are drawn out of what we already know and must be coherent with it. We cannot offer a vision of heaven that contradicts our prior claims about God, humanity, creation, redemption, and so on. This means that theological reflections on heaven balance between the constant recognition of our lack of knowledge and a commitment to what knowledge we do have. "I don't know much, but this much I know."

Shawnthea: As a pastor, I think about heaven quite a bit. It's fun to sit and ponder the afterlife, exploring the theological contours and byways, picking at the tangled knots left by conflicting biblical accounts. (Is heaven a house? Or more like Eden? Or just a suburban landscape, as depicted in those colorful tracts handed out door-to-door?) Plus, it's an excellent form of theological exercise to make a statement about heaven and test to see if it coheres with everything else I say about the Christian faith. Yet, like any good theologians, pastors have to admit that anything we say about heaven is pure speculation. We just don't know.

For as much time as I spend wondering about heaven, it's surprising how rarely the subject comes up in the day to day. It doesn't come up in Bible study, no one mentions it as one of the pressing questions of faith, and I have yet to have someone come to my office troubled with concerns about the afterlife. Perhaps this is because talk of heaven presumes death, and we are a death-denying culture. Everyday life in the United States is not particularly threatening. Life expectancy is at an all-time high for most Americans, so from a medical point of view, death represents failure.

But then the day comes. There is an accident, a diagnosis, a sudden change, or a slow decline. Eventually we reach the limits of luck or medicine and healing is not an option. When the infinite horizon of the future becomes finite and the end is visible, everyone wonders about heaven.

Like theologians, pastors are bound when speaking of heaven, but the restraints are relational, not theological. In ministry, my primary job is to give spiritual care to people, especially in times of need. What I will say in the emergency room or standing at the graveside may bear little resemblance to what I would say in the classroom. In a crisis, theological nuance and doctrinal purity must sometimes be sacrificed for the sake of compassion. Furthermore, whatever doubts or debates I entertain in my office disappear at the bedside of a dying person. And in that moment, the question "Will I go to heaven?" has but one answer: "Yes, yes, a thousand times yes!"

When we decided to write this chapter, I suggested we ask my parishioners if they had any thoughts or questions on the subject. Given the seeming lack of interest, I didn't expect very much, but the response was amazing. For as little as we discuss heaven in church, it is clear that many people are wondering and worrying about it on their own. Some of the questions were funny, others thoughtful, others touching. Yet they all revealed a deep longing to know more, not just about heaven, but about the nature of God, the limits of forgiveness, and the power of love. These deeper questions frame my responses.

Time and Eternity

What do we do in heaven? —*Christine*

Do we spend eternity just with those we love, or is it one endless cocktail party with millions of souls? —*Paul*

I don't want to do anything. I'd prefer just to fall into a dreamless sleep. Isn't that reward enough? —*Pam*

Shannon: One of the theological limitations of our knowledge, and even our imagination, about heaven is the difficulty of understanding the relationship between time and eternity. Some theologians contend that time itself is part of creation, such that temporality is a characteristic of creation, but not of eternity. In this view, eternal life is not an infinite extension of time; it is not everlasting. It is, instead, eternal, meaning that it is not temporal. All of our experience is temporal. Time is one of the basic conditions of human experience and human knowledge. How can we begin to imagine a reality that is not? All of our words and concepts are time-bound, such that even when we try to visualize or describe eternity, we use temporal ideas to do so. Eternity is permanent, always true, never ending. These are temporal phrases, clumsily pointing toward a reality outside of time.

Theologians offer different understandings of the relationship between time and eternity. Karl Barth, a twentieth-century Protestant theologian, imagines time as an island floating on the endless ocean of eternity. Karl Rahner, a twentieth-century Roman Catholic theologian, says that eternity is the mature fruit of time, provocatively suggesting that while time is born of eternity, the eternal comes to be in time. No theologian has perfectly captured a completely persuasive vision of the relationship between time and eternity. However, the struggle to do so shapes our views of heaven, as we often tend toward temporal understandings that may not apply to eternal realities.

The relationship of time to eternity is important in questions about what we do in heaven. If heaven is an endless, never-ending expanse of time, won't we be bored silly? If heaven is an eternity outside of time, does that mean it will be always the same? It is hard to imagine change of any kind without time, since change implies before and after. Eternal life without any change or growth also seems like a boring prospect.

And what about conflict? The key to dramatic interest is conflict, which generates suspense and makes room for surprise. "Happily ever after" is the end of the story, not the juicy part that keeps us on the edge of our seats. As much as we aspire to see clearly and know fully, won't that make heaven rather dull?

Here we must remember what we don't know and what we do. We do not know what eternity will be like. We do know something about God. As Trinity, God is relational and dynamic. In Jesus, God enters history and fully partakes of human conflict. In the Spirit, God is the source of endless creativity, serendipity, and surprise. As difficult as it is to imagine endless time as exciting, or growth without temporality, it is even more difficult to imagine the God of Christianity as static. It may well be that the resolution of the drama is the most exciting part.

Thus my direct answer to these questions is, of course, I don't know. However, I would also say this: I find God to be fascinating, challenging, overwhelming, annoying, and wildly surprising. What little I know of God and grace in this life assures me that God is never boring, and heaven won't be either.

Shawnthea: Our curiosity about what we will do in heaven is part of living in the world. We are all about the *doing*, and doing requires time. Even the desire for heaven to be a dreamless sleep is a worldly, time-bound response. We can't imagine doing anything, even something we enjoy, for an eternity. Better just to sleep.

But what if heaven is not about doing but *being*? Shannon opens up a whole new possibility in her discussion of time and eternity. Creation is bounded by time—the doing—but heaven is loosed from those bonds. Heaven could be a state of being.

We spend our lives hoping for times of peace and happiness and contentment. These are not things we do but states of being. A state of being doesn't require time; it just is. My quick definition of heaven is to be in the presence of God. That is where we find the peace that passes all understanding. If we are in such a state of contented bliss, what we do is irrelevant. We will *be* with God at last.

Body and Soul

When we die, do we become ghosts, a misty semblance of our earthly selves, or are we new creatures with bodies? —Mary

Do we have form in heaven, or are we just spirits? And if we have form, will it look like us? —Tim

What age will I be in heaven? If my mother is there, how will I recognize her? —Gina

Shannon: Mainstream Christianity affirms the resurrection of the body. As I have said many times, Christianity is a multiple and fluid tradition that includes a wide variety of different Christian communities across time and space. Within this multiplicity, some Christian communities have claimed that the soul is immortal, rather than that the whole person is resurrected. Yet on the whole, the tradition has clung to the difficult doctrine of bodily resurrection. It would be much easier, philosophically, to make a sharp, dualistic divide between the soul and the body and claim only that the soul does not die. The soul "shuffles off this mortal coil," leaves the husk behind, and ascends to a spiritual realm. This makes a lot of theological muddles much clearer and easier to resolve. Several of the questions we received from parishioners regarding heaven disappear if we do not have to deal with bodies. Where is heaven? How old will I be in heaven? These questions evaporate if we are only spirits. Also, larger theological puzzles, such as why evil exists and how redemption happens, are vastly simplified if bodies have no eternal significance.

And yet the main line of Christianity affirms the resurrection of the body. This is the harder road to travel philosophically. It raises a lot of questions, prevents easy answers, and means that the various messy realities of embodied life cannot be dismissed. The affirmation of bodily resurrection is also in perfect keeping with the Christian story. The narratives of Jesus Christ are fleshy through and through. The cast of this drama is filled with characters whose embodiment is hard to overlook: a pregnant woman, a crying infant, lepers, prostitutes, a blind man, a bleeding woman, manual laborers, dying children and friends, prisoners in midexecution. In chapter 1, I wrote of how, during the early modern period, people in the West began to see the human person primarily as a rational, autonomous subject. Remember Descartes's "I think, therefore I am." That view of humanity contrasts sharply with what is found in biblical narratives. The cast of this drama is not made up of interchangeable, individual thinkers, but fleshy people, for whom embodied relationships and experience are primary to identity. Thus it is not surprising that bodies matter in Christianity, now and always. The God who became incarnate, enfleshed, is not only interested in our minds, spirits, and souls. The God of Jesus Christ redeems and resurrects the whole person, which is embodied.

Of course, this strong theological affirmation (what we do know) is paired with a heavy dose of epistemic humility (what we don't know). We have a lot of experience of embodiment, and we have professions and disciplines that study the human body in depth. Yet we still know little about the human body. Indeed, some of the most advanced research on human bodies reminds us that we have a lot to learn. Human bodies are open systems, such that we are deeply affected physically by relationships to other human beings. One example of this is adoptive mothers, whose bodies go through hormonal changes similar to those of women who have just given birth. The physical and chemical changes are stimulated not by pregnancy and childbirth, but by caring for an infant.[1] Stress, fear, love, nurture—all of these interpersonal, relational realities—influence us physically, often with permanent results. In a different way, our bodies are open systems to the entire universe.[2]

Given that we do not fully know or understand our own bodies here and now, and given that resurrection involves not just change but profound transformation, we do not know what embodiment will mean in heaven. We do not know. As a theologian, then, my answer to the question of whether we will be bodies or just spirits in heaven is twofold. We will be embodied. We do not know what that will mean or look like.

Shawnthea: As a pastor, I am a staunch defender of the bodily resurrection of Jesus. There is too much at stake for me to surrender *that* body to the grave. First, the resurrection of the body is the ultimate vindication of Jesus' life and ministry. The world says "no" by executing Jesus, but God says "yes" by bringing that same person back to life. More than that, the bodily resurrection has implications for creation. If in death Jesus sheds all signs of the incarnation and comes back only as spirit, then the material things of this world have less value. It is a dangerous dualism that puts spiritual issues ahead of physical or "creaturely" issues, weakening the demands of the gospel in regard to the things of this world. But if Christ's body was resurrected along with his spirit, then God has hallowed creation by raising a part of it.

From my point of view, if Jesus did not resurrect in bodily form, I think I'd do better to stay in bed on Sundays. Yet for all my certainty about Christ's resurrection, I'm unsure about precisely what that means for us after we die. Even the witness of Scripture offers a variety of answers.

We know that Jesus came back, but it was not obvious that it was him. Mary, tearfully emerging from the empty tomb, meets Jesus and thinks he's the gardener (John 20:14-17). Doesn't he look like himself? What sort of body is this? After hearing him call her by name, Mary recognizes that the stranger is Jesus, and she makes a move to hug him, but Jesus says, "Do not hold on to me, because I have not yet ascended to the Father."

On the road to Emmaus, two of the disciples walk some distance with Jesus, never once suspecting their wise companion is the risen Christ (Luke 24:13-35). They recognize him only when he takes the familiar role as host and breaks the bread for them. In that instant they recognize him and he vanishes. What sort of body is this that can break bread *and* pass through walls (John 20:19, 26)? It is Jesus and yet not Jesus. Is this what we will be like, ourselves and yet not ourselves? Will we be recognizable as ourselves but only to those who knew us? It is a mystery.

Yet I am content to let this remain a mystery—just as I am willing to accept the mystery of Christ's resurrection. Jesus rose from the dead, and he promised that all would rise with him.[3]

Do we become angels in heaven? —Mary

Shannon: Popular culture often suggests that we will become angels in heaven. I cannot resist the opportunity to refute this. Angels and humans are fundamentally different, precisely because humans are embodied. Angels are not corporeal, embodied creatures. Human beings who go to heaven are saved, redeemed, and resurrected into eternal life precisely as human beings. We do not become another kind of creature altogether.

Shawnthea: I have to disagree with Shannon on this point, and I do so not because I think her theology is invalid but because when it comes to the question of angels, the stakes are different. Like a good theologian, I know there is a fundamental difference between humans and angels, but as a pastor, I also know the subject of angels is a loaded one—for even Jesus says we will be "like angels in heaven" (Mark 12:25). In answering, I let the questioner lead me. Some people take great comfort in the idea that loved ones have become angels and, like Clarence in *It's a Wonderful Life*, have "gotten their wings." In the face of great loss, there is even something redemptive in the idea that the dead are given a new role to play in our lives. True, the theology may be unsound, but what crucial point of theology is at stake here? It seems like theological nitpicking. When someone has experienced a devastating loss, angels may offer more comfort than correct theology.

Of course, not everyone finds this comforting, which is why pastors must tread carefully. I sat with a young girl whose father had died after a brief battle with liver cancer. At the funeral a dear soul took the girl's hand and said, "God must have needed a special angel in heaven." The daughter glared back and said, "God should know I needed him here!" She took no comfort in the suggestion that her father had received a divine promotion.

On the other hand, when I was once asked, "Is my daughter an angel now?" I knew the mother was not looking for robust theology but for some scrap of comfort to which she could cling in the midst of devastating loss. Theologians know the correct answer is no. Pastors know the right answer is yes. With conviction in my voice, I answered, "Yes, she is. She is glorious and perfect and in the presence of God."

Shannon: I'll accept the accusation that my response to the question of angels is theological nitpicking from Shawnthea, but only because I know she is a staunch believer in bodily resurrection. My worry about imagining that humans become angels in heaven is really a concern that bodily resurrection is lost and heaven is seen in purely spiritual terms.

The How and the Who

Is heaven the "eternal reward," and if so, a reward for what? —Janet

If Jesus is the only way to heaven, what about the people who died before he began his ministry? —June

How good do I have to be to get to heaven? —Paul

Shannon: To answer these questions, I need to reiterate some of the things explored in chapter 3, where I discussed some similarities and differences between Reformed Protestant and Roman Catholic theologies. These two groups would answer these questions differently.

From a Reformed Protestant perspective, any understanding of who gets to heaven or how they get there must begin with the affirmation that salvation is the work of God. We are finite and fallen, and we cannot accomplish our own salvation. We cannot, for Reformed Protestants, contribute to our salvation in any way. This means that "who goes" is entirely decided by God, without regard to our actions or beliefs. God chooses who goes to heaven, and this choice is not predicated on God's knowledge of our past, present, or future behavior. It is God's good pleasure.

Once you affirm that salvation is entirely up to God with no human participation, there are only a few logical options for understanding who gets to heaven. The first is double predestination. God sends some people to heaven and some people to hell, without regard for their actions or beliefs. The second is single predestination. This says that we all are sinful and fallen, deserving of eternal damnation. God chooses to elect some people to salvation and does not do anything regarding the eternal state of others, those who are not elect. Quite frankly, given God's omnipotence, I find this to be philosophically unsatisfying. It is a way of trying to get God off the hook for those who go to hell. But if we are all sinful and the omnipotent God chooses to save some, that seems very close to God choosing to damn others. The third option is universal salvation. This, again, affirms that God ordains salvation for some without regard to their beliefs or actions, but boldly claims that we all are included in that gracious act. God saves everyone.

Roman Catholic theology also begins all conversations about who goes to heaven with the affirmation that salvation is the work of God. We can in no way save ourselves. However, Roman Catholic theology also has space for human participation in our salvation, always noting that this participation is enabled by and reliant upon the grace of God.

Karl Rahner says that God offers to each of us God's own self-communication. God offers us grace. This grace is a vocation to beatific vision. This offer is not like someone offering you dessert after dinner, which you could equally accept or reject. ("Would you like a slice of pie?" "No, thanks." And the exchange is over.) Instead, God graciously ordains humanity to a supernatural end, in such a way that this ordination is the truest thing about us. Whether we say yes or no to God's offer, we will always and irrevocably be people to whom God has offered grace. We most truly are people who are called into heaven. With God's enabling grace, we can accept our own identity as such, or we can deny this truth of who we are, willfully distort ourselves, and stubbornly refuse this gift. Our refusal does not change God's mind about us or mean that God rescinds the offer. It changes us, perversely contorting us into knots of self-deception.

How do we say yes or no to God's grace? For Rahner, we say yes by being open to the unknown other, both human and divine. Put more simply, we say yes by loving God and neighbor. When Rahner talks about love, he does not mean romantic emotional attachment (although that can be a part of it), but rather the moments, large and small, when we see the other person as her own person, not a reflection of ourselves or someone who can fulfill our needs—moments when we are loyal, although no one would judge us for abandoning the other; moments when we do our duty by our neighbors, even though no one is watching and no one will know. The love that Rahner writes about is personal, social, political. It is the million times throughout our lives when we make choices that would make no sense if there were no God. Whether or not we think of it as a religious decision, when we act as if the ultimate meaning of the world is good, rather than neutral, this is love. When we act as if there is meaning to this world beyond what human society understands and rewards, this is faith. When we act as if the world is a place of grace and redemption, even though there is precious little evidence of this in the daily news, this is hope. These are some of the ways that we say yes to God.[4]

How do we say no? By refusing to say yes. When we choose not to love God and neighbor, to close ourselves off from others, to see both God and neighbor as means to our own ends, we are saying no to God's offer of eternal grace.

For Rahner, this choice of accepting or refusing God's grace is made over the course of an entire lifetime. Because our own actions always take place within a context of sin, and are therefore also always sinful, and because our own knowledge—even of ourselves—is so limited, we never know for sure if we are saying yes or no. We hope for our own salvation only within the hope for salvation for all of humanity, clinging to the steadfast grace of God.

It is important to note that while Rahner speaks within a framework of institutional Christianity, is deeply committed to the church, and expects those who hear the good news of Christianity to become committed, churchgoing Christians, his description of how we say yes or no to God is not about church membership, creedal beliefs, or sacraments. He affirms a traditional theological view that God offers salvation to all people and goes further to affirm that while all salvation ultimately comes through Jesus Christ, other religions can have salvific importance to people. Someone can be saved as a Buddhist, Muslim, secular humanist, and so on. The God who saves them, for Rahner, does so through the grace of Jesus Christ. However, the person who is saved need not know of, believe in, or accept Jesus as savior. Grace is offered to all, in and through Jesus. When individuals obey their consciences and love their neighbor, they say yes to God and accept this grace.

Discussing Rahner's view of heaven raises the question of his view of hell. God, as described in Rahner's theology, loves each of us and offers us all grace. There is no place of punishment to which a God of wrath condemns those who are rejected. However, there is the real possibility that some people never say yes to God and close themselves off from God and neighbor such that their reality becomes one of self-distorting deception. Hell, then, would be to be held in eternal existence by God, who loves you, while you deny this truth and reject the love of God. For some people, this is so far from the fire-and-brimstone vision of hell as punishment that it is hard to recognize it as hell. Yet I find the concept of eternal self-seclusion in a reality that rejects all love to be truly terrifying. Other people are quick to think that Rahner believes all people will be saved, since he believes that God loves all people. Rahner did hope for universal salvation. However, he was also too aware of how little we know and how high the stakes are on this matter to assert that salvation is universal. Human freedom and dignity are so honored by God that they have eternal consequences. Who and how we choose to be in our lives play a role in determining our eternal fate. For a theologian to say blithely that everyone is saved is, from a Rahnerian view, irresponsible, since it speaks beyond our knowledge and might harm someone by convincing him that his choices do not matter.

While Rahner's view of hell is not one of punishment, neither is his view of heaven that of a reward. The notion of reward implies that we get something we deserve for good behavior. In contrast, eternal salvation is a gift beyond anything we could merit. It is grace: an unexacted, unearned gift from God. Rahner does say our actions matter regarding whether we get to heaven or not. However, this earthly life is not a testing ground for something that comes later, and heaven and hell are not a carrot and stick to keep us in line. Rather, God creates human beings with the dignity of freedom. We get to—and have to—make choices. Through these choices, over the course of our lifetimes, we participate in crafting our own identities. We can become people who accept the love of God and live with love for others. Or we can become people who reject the love of God and close ourselves off from true encounters with others. We can obey our consciences, live by higher lights than selfish gain, and step into our own God-given vocation to be children of God. Or we can ignore our consciences, strive for our own imagined pleasures, and never recognize that we are chosen and loved by the Creator of the universe. Our identities are then shaped by God's love for us and our response to that love. And these identities, created in time, are who we are for all eternity.

Because of this relationship between time and eternity, it would be foolish to imagine that one should overlook present sufferings in light of the promise of heaven. To ignore injustices now, in hopes of better things in eternity, is to misunderstand how eternity comes to be. In the loving of others—especially those who suffer or are oppressed—we choose to accept our vocation as God's children, destined for eternal life. The hope for heaven does not diminish the importance of earthly, temporal life. Indeed, it does the opposite in Rahner's view, granting eternal validity to the freedom exercised here and now. At the same time, we are surrounded by suffering and evils that, as far as we can see, are unredeemed in this lifetime. Hope in the resurrection and in heaven allows us to affirm that such suffering will be redeemed in the life to come, through the grace of God.

Shawnthea: Let me get my cards out on the table. First, I am a Protestant, and my response to all these questions is rooted in that tradition. Second, I believe that Jesus Christ revealed the true nature of God—God is ultimately loving and means for us to have life and have it abundantly. In my opinion, the God who loves us enough to take human form must also love us too much to send anyone to hell. Therefore, I believe in universal salvation. We all rise (John 12:32). This is not a commonly held belief, and I know there are biblical and theological warrants that would lead to other answers, but I believe universal salvation fits with what I know of Jesus Christ.

But there's something about universal salvation that bothers people. Take, for example, the laborers in Matthew (20:1-16) who are insulted that the landowner has paid everyone the same, or the elder brother of the prodigal son, who resents the extravagant welcome his father extends to his no-good brother (Luke 15:11-32). We want to believe we deserve to go to heaven, but we're equally sure there are others who do not merit such a reward.

These questions about heaven are rooted in human categories such as "deserve" and "merit." Eventually we all become like the lawyer in Luke's account who cuts to the chase and asks Jesus, "What must I do to inherit eternal life?" (Luke 10:25). Exploring the theological terrain of heaven is all fine and good, but at the end of the day, what we really want is a "to do" list. But there is no list, no set of tasks that, once accomplished, guarantees salvation and puts our minds at ease. And even if there were such a list, we couldn't do it. We're just not capable. The question "How good do I have to be?" is easily answered: "Better than you can be." If our salvation was in our hands, hell would be standing room only.

So what can we do? Admit that our salvation is out of our hands and in the hands of God who, in mercy and love, has saved us. Then live a life worthy of such an astonishing gift. In other words, I know I am a sinner, but I believe that God, through Jesus Christ, has saved me. For this reason, I am filled with gratitude and love—love for God and love for neighbor. Heaven is not a reward for a well-lived life. Rather, salvation is the beginning of a life well lived.

Universal salvation also solves the problem of who gets into heaven. There is no need to put pencil to paper and figure out what to do with those born before the time of Jesus, nor do we have to lose sleep over those who were not baptized or those who never had a chance to hear the good news. God will deal with all people as God has dealt with us—mercifully.

This is not to say that grace is cheap or that baptism is not sacramental or that there is no need to evangelize. There is nothing cheap about this grace if we properly understand what God has done for us. Such a gift ought to reorient our lives in powerful ways, setting us on a journey of service in Christ's name. As for baptism, this remains the sacrament through which we are brought into the body of Christ, which is a new way of life, a life nurtured in the church and lived in community. This is the life abundant, so rich and meaningful that we ought to tell everyone we meet what God has done.

Here and Now

Can we experience heaven now? —Mary

Is heaven a time and place or a state of being? —Mark

Shannon: Christian theologians have very different views on these questions. Some see heaven as existing only at the end of time. Others hold to a view called "realized eschatology," in which all that will happen at the end of time is already present here and now. Many theologians, myself included, fall in between these two views, relying on the biblical witness that the new creation has already been inaugurated in Jesus Christ but is not yet fully realized. The "already/not yet" means that we can participate in the new creation in fragmentary ways, while we are aware that the fullness of eschatological consummation is not yet something we can know or experience.

The Protestant theologian Letty Russell writes about living "proleptically." Something is anachronistic when it is from the past and has been displaced into the present. For example, imagine contemporary NASA scientists calculating using slide rules. Conversely, something is proleptic when it is from the future and has been displaced into the present. Russell says that Jesus is a "memory of the future."[5] Looking back in time to Jesus, we can see the characteristics of the ultimate future, the new creation. This makes it possible for us to live proleptically—to live as if the future were already here.[6] Thus, in moments of faithful living, we proleptically experience the taste of the new creation.

Rahner uses a different framework and terminology to express something similar. Since eternity comes to be in time, and heaven specifically through the moments when we say yes to God, then when we do say yes in loving God and neighbor, we participate in eternity here and now.[7]

Both Rahner and Russell look forward to a full realization of the new creation in the eschaton. Both also perceive ways in which we can participate in heaven—in glimpses or moments—within our present earthly life.

Shawnthea: Floating in a hot tub overlooking the Gulf Coast, I said, "This is heaven!" Why do we use that word? Since we know nothing of the afterlife, what does it mean when we say something is *heavenly*? In my case it meant a sense of total peace, complete contentment, and delight in all of creation. There is something within us that yearns for these moments, moments that are so rare and yet so deeply satisfying that we hope the next life is more of the same. If we're talking only about the peace that passes all understanding, then I think it is possible to experience something akin to heaven now.

What if we think about heaven more along the lines of "thy kingdom come, thy will be done"? Is it possible to experience that here and now? I say yes. There is another kind of peace and contentment that comes not from physical pleasure, but from living in a way that is synchronistic with the will of God. Shannon describes this as saying yes to God and neighbor, and I find this answer compelling. Anyone who has discerned a call and pursued it has tasted a bit of this kind of heaven. But there is another angle to be considered.

One man submitted a concern, rather than a question. He wrote, "A minister I know says that heaven and hell are here and now; there is nothing else, so we shouldn't waste our time contemplating the sweet by-and-by. I find this thought disturbing." I tend to agree. This "here and now" view of heaven (and hell) is a popular idea among bright, well-intentioned Christians who are committed to social activism. It serves two purposes: First, it keeps people from being distracted from the real issues of the day by thoughts of heaven. Second, it puts some teeth in the demands of the social gospel, calling people to act lest heaven slip away. Here is where the trouble lies for me, for this claim bears a close resemblance to the more conservative, instrumentalist view of heaven. "Do the right thing or you won't *get* to heaven" is not so different from "Do the right thing or this won't *be* heaven." Either way, heaven becomes a reward for right action, whether it's now or later. While I am in favor of any view that keeps Christians engaged in real life, I find the "here and now" theory of salvation problematic, especially when it goes in a direction that suggests we have the power to save ourselves. Beyond that, I am persuaded that the apostle Paul is onto something when he writes, "If for this life only we have hoped in Christ, we are of all people most to be pitied" (1 Cor. 15:19).

Recognition and Reconciliation

Will I see my mom and stepfather again? —Gina

Will I recognize my sister who died in infancy? —Dawn

Will you see people who have hurt you in heaven? Or do dysfunctional relationships mend? —Rachel

Shannon: Answering again from a Rahnerian perspective, I would say that relationships are integral to the identity we craft during our lifetimes and to the process by which we say yes to God. What is preserved in heavenly eternity is precisely the love, faith, and hope that we enact during our lifetimes—all three of which happen within relationships. We accept our grace-given identity as those who are called to heaven by God precisely in loving relationships. These relationships, then, are profoundly part of who we are. To say that "we" are preserved in heaven is to say that these relationships are preserved.

This is very much in keeping with contemporary views of the human person, many of which focus on the ways in which who we are comes to be over time, in and through our cultural and social relationships. I could not begin to describe who I am without talking about the people and experiences in my life that have shaped me. If you have read the rest of this book, you know a lot about me. I am a middle-class white woman who grew up in West Virginia and has been educated in the Ivy League. I am a teacher of students; friend of Shawnthea; reader of Rahner; mother of Jacob, Elias, and Lucy; wife of Seth; and lover of Jesus. My identity is—to some degree or another—socially constructed.

This casts the question in a somewhat different light. If the relationships that have formed me, and that are so much a part of me, are not preserved, how could I be preserved? Wouldn't I cease to be me?

While both a Rahnerian perspective and contemporary views of the self lead to a clear affirmation that if we are preserved in heaven, our relationships are preserved, this in turn leads to some tricky theological questions. As one parishioner wrote, "What about the bad relationships?" What about the relationships of violence and oppression? The relationships of loss, or the relationships that never came to be? If all of these painful relationships are—like the joyful ones—part of our identities, how could they be excluded from heaven without excluding huge parts of us?

Years ago an undergraduate, Tirzah Enumah, wrote a short fictional story for one of my classes that illustrated this theological thicket quite beautifully. She wrote of Jeehae, who had been a Korean comfort woman. Kidnapped as an adolescent, she had been forced into years of sexual slavery. When Jeehae awakens on her first day in heaven, she faces both joy and confusion. She meets her mother, who never knew what happened to her child. Does she tell her mother—blissfully ignorant—about the horrors she endured? She cannot bring herself to speak the truth. Jeehae meets other people who are joyfully reunited with their children. Although Jeehae had always wanted to be a mother, the violence done to her body rendered her infertile. She never knew the joys of parenthood, never gained the identity of "mother." Instead, the loss of motherhood is part of who she is. Jeehae's identity has been radically shaped by horrendous evil.[8] How can that evil be redeemed without erasing Jeehae's identity, without erasing who she is? Jesus offers to relieve Jeehae of her sorrow. "'No!' Jeehae exclaimed, abruptly jerking her hand away from His. She bolted to her feet, spinning to face Jesus. 'It may be awful, but it's mine. If you take this away from me, what else do I have? This is who I am; for the decades after my experience, my anguish consumed me. I have nothing—I am no one—without these memories.'"[9]

If our identities are socially constructed, and some of the relationships and experiences that form us are painful, what happens to that pain in heaven? The Bible says that every tear shall be wiped away.[10] What if those tears are part of who we are? Are we wiped away, in some sense?

Some argue that heaven must involve some forgetting on our part.[11] I find Rahner's theological affirmations of the eternal significance of earthly life to be profound and persuasive. I also find current descriptions of the self as socially constructed to be convincing. Therefore, I am hesitant to imagine a heaven of forgetfulness, where the worst parts of life are erased from memory. Instead, I hope boldly in the power of God to transform and redeem even the horrendous elements of human existence. Here I follow the work of contemporary theologian and philosopher Marilyn Adams. In her writings, Adams looks closely at the depth and breadth of human involvement in suffering and evil. She does not flinch from the sight of it, diminish its significance, or try to keep God's hands clean from the mess. Rather, she faithfully demands and expects that the resurrection of Jesus Christ means that even the worst that the world has to offer will be joyfully transformed by the overwhelming power of the goodness of God.[12]

As far as I can tell, the God of Jesus Christ often does not prevent horrible things from happening to us. God shows up, but not Hollywood-style, not in the nick of time to prevent tragedy from striking. Instead, God shows up days later, after the pain has been endured, the breaking point is past, and the body has begun to stink in the grave. Then when any human sense of time proclaims that it is far too late for good news, God arrives. And somehow, in the contact with God's grace, the horrors of the past are not merely erased; they are transformed. After Easter we do not forget the crucifixion. The identity of the risen Christ is still that of the Crucified One. My hope for heaven is for that kind of resurrection joy in which our identities and our relationships are preserved and transformed by the grace of God.

Shawnthea: When it comes to questions of recognition and reconciliation, I find we are too much with this world. Even the response of the theologians is firmly rooted in the unchallenged importance of human experience as ultimately defining. Don't get me wrong— I believe individual experience is critically important to our self-understanding. In this life, theories of identity construction are fascinating and useful. And after all, the incarnation took a specific form, Jesus of Nazareth, not a generic form. But when it comes to thinking about heaven, I think our attachment to our identities is distracting.

I am reminded of Jesus and the Sadducees who try to discredit the idea of the resurrection with the story of the woman with seven husbands (Matt. 22:23-30; Mark 12:18-25; Luke 20:27-35). The unlucky bride marries seven brothers in succession, according to the Levirate marriage law, and the Sadducees ask whose wife she will be in heaven. Jesus answers, "Those who belong to this age marry and are given in marriage; but those who are considered worthy of a place in that age and in the resurrection from the dead neither marry nor are given in marriage" (Luke 20:34-35). In other words, human relationships may not take the same form after the resurrection.

This is not to say that human experience is irrelevant after death. If there is a heaven, I believe we are still ourselves. Nor do I take what happens in this life lightly or gloss over the hardships, suffering, and loss. All our experiences, good and bad, shape and define us as people. Nor do I believe we forget, as if heaven were some form of sanctified, selective Alzheimer's. Instead, I believe that our capacity to love expands exponentially. That's the power of entering into the presence of God, when we will finally, as Paul describes, "see face to face. Now I know only in part; then I will know fully, even as I have been fully known" (1 Cor. 13:12). Once we have entered into the presence of God, perhaps we become able to bear what we could not bear in this life. What we could not face, we can face without shame or sorrow. Those whom we could not love, we can finally love. Yes, we remain the people we were in life, but with a greater capacity to love.

Having said all this, I'm now going to backtrack—and here's why. So far I've answered these questions in a vacuum. But questions about recognition and reconciliation in the afterlife are never without context. There is a face; there is a voice; there is a loved one who is missing and missed. Or in the case of reconciliation, there is a wound or a broken relationship that has never been mended or accounted for. Even when these questions are asked in an abstract form, a pastor would do well to remember that the questioner is looking over your shoulder, hoping to catch a glimpse of a particular face. So if a widow asks me if she will see her husband again in heaven, I would never quote Jesus, "The dead neither marry nor are given in marriage." I would probably say, "Yes." Given how little we know of heaven, this may be true. Whether I am right or wrong, in the end, I doubt it will matter.

Leaving the side of the widow for a moment, let's think of this more broadly. If we believe that the love we have experienced in this life has given us a glimpse of what God is truly like, then when we die, we will be in the presence of a love that is beyond our power of imagination, a love so powerful and all-consuming that it holds every breathtaking moment in this life. Immersed in this love, in this God, we will either meet our loved ones again or be so content and at peace that it won't matter.

The same is true for those relationships that have been broken or painful. Love is going to win in the end. It's like childbirth. I remember that in Lamaze class all the first-time mothers were fixated on pain and pain management. One young woman worried that if the pain was too much, she would resent her newborn child. The midwife reassured her, "Once you get a look at that baby, everything but love will melt away." So it will be in heaven. The last stanza of Charles Wesley's hymn "Love Divine, All Loves Excelling" puts it well.

> Finish, then, Thy new creation,
> Pure and spotless let us be;
> Let us see Thy great salvation
> Perfectly restored in Thee:
> Changed from glory into glory,
> Till in heav'n we take our place,
> Till we cast our crowns before Thee,
> Lost in wonder, love, and praise.[13]

Influence of the Dead

Can people in heaven see what's going on? Can they influence our lives? —Karen

Shannon: This question touches on the subject of when heaven happens. After we die do we wait until the end of time for the general resurrection? This would place us all in a situation like the one described by Thornton Wilder in the play *Our Town*. Or does each of us go to heaven right away? Much of the Christian tradition affirms that heaven is an eschatological reality, in the sense that it comes to be at the end of time with the general resurrection of all those who are saved. Yet Rahner and others suggest that it makes sense to imagine each person entering heaven upon death, since eternity is not something that starts after time ends, but rather a reality that surrounds all of time.[14] Since I am offering theology influenced by Rahner in this chapter, I will assume, in answering this question, that each person enters heaven when he or she dies.

Like every other question about heaven, this one must first be answered by "I don't know." Then we have to remember some of the theological constraints, such as the difficulties of understanding time and eternity. I would be very hesitant to imagine that those who have died are still existing in time and therefore interacting in temporal ways. I would be hesitant to credit Aunt Mary with pulling someone back on the sidewalk just before the reckless driver turned the corner, or to give any affirmation involving those who have died looking down through a glass floor to see and intervene in temporal affairs.

At the same time, I do want to affirm that loving relationships matter—eternally—and are part of our faithful relationships with God. We are social beings, created by a triune God, living our faith in community. Imagine someone who loved you has died and said yes to God. Indeed, her loving you is part of her saying yes to God—the part of her faith that participates in eternity. She is in communion with God, the creator and sustainer of the universe. Her love for you is only stronger after death, a kind of pure prayer directly to God on your behalf, the love between you becoming part of the fabric of heaven. How could that not affect you?

There might be moments when a person, here and now, interprets her experience of such powerful love in temporal ways, seeing her departed mother with her on her wedding day or feeling her deceased father's arms around her in a moment of crisis. Unless understood terribly literally, such experiences seem to me to be faithful affirmation of the reality of the communion of the saints, encouraging us always.

Shawnthea: I prefer the answer "I don't know" because it saves me from having to explain the communion of the saints, explore the thin place between life and death, or face some of the miraculous encounters I have witnessed. Perhaps a better response is to ask, "Why does it matter?" Let's think about this in a different way. For example, if your long-dead grandfather can see you, how does that change your life? Do you gain a sense of comfort, safety, or peace from the idea that your loved one continues to watch over you? Or would you behave better knowing that he was watching? My mother used to call out to me before I left the house as a teenager, "Don't do anything you wouldn't want me to see." Her words had a dampening effect on my social life, which was her intent. Whatever effect this has on us, sorting out whether the dead play this role in our lives is somewhat beside the point because we do believe that God is watching over us and has the power to influence us. As the psalmist sings:

O LORD, you have searched me and known me.
You know when I sit down and when I rise up;
    you discern my thoughts from far away.
You search out my path and my lying down,
    and are acquainted with all my ways."

Psalm 139:1-3

We may not know how many are watching over us, but we know there is at least One.

Having said that it doesn't matter so much if our loved ones watch over us if it is just God, I have a confession to make. At times I have felt spiritually bereft and empty, abandoned by God. In those wilderness moments, I have prayed to my grandmother Grace, the most joyful and faithful Christian I've ever known, someone I can picture seated in the company of the saints. And every time, those prayers have brought me back to faith. I'm sure that Grace is in heaven, but does she look like I remember her? Is she watching over me? There may be some theologically correct answer, but when I am trying to find my way back to God, imagining Grace's smiling face works wonders.

Location

If Jesus is in heaven, and he told us, "I am with you always," does that mean heaven is near? Or is it distant, as in the prayer, "Our Father, who art in heaven"? —Mary

Where is heaven? —Dick

Shannon: Once again, I don't know. When I try to imagine space without time, my head hurts. Unless we are moving into science fiction, we cannot begin to make geographical claims about eternity, inhabited by embodied, resurrected persons in communion with God. I do not know. And that is okay. I do not need to know where heaven is located. I am not planning to get there on my own. Christian faith is not about certainty. It is a relationship of love, held in faith, lived in hope, all in and through the grace of God. Any guess I would make about where heaven might be would have to be a simple extrapolation of the experience of grace. So when my children ask, "Where is heaven?" I answer, "Even closer to God than we are."

Shawnthea: Amen.

Living Conversation

This project began with our desire to share the excitement and insight we find in our conversations when the work of the academy and the work of the church come together. We wanted to share our dialogue and encourage others to start their own theological conversations. Yet merely transcribing our talks together failed to capture the dynamic give-and-take that marks our conversations about theology. How could we communicate the energy generated by our heated debates about the role of the church? What words could describe the gales of laughter that surrounded our discussion of communion practices? On the page, what once lived and breathed, pulsing with the Spirit, became static. As with a butterfly pinned and fixed for display, you may be able to study the object more closely, but without movement, it becomes dry and one-dimensional. No, a transcript would not do the trick.

It is precisely the ongoing fluidity, the multiplicity, and the movement of our dialogue that is so much fun, and these characteristics stem more from the subject than the form. Pastors and theologians both know that theology doesn't hold still. It is a field that can move and breathe, responding to the ever-changing circumstances of Christian life and new ways of thinking. This makes perfect sense if Christian theology is seen as a way of understanding how and why people relate to and engage with the living God.

We wanted to convey the living movement of theology more than we wanted to preserve the form of our conversations, so we tried to find ways we could hold still different theological doctrines long enough to study them, while also allowing room for movement and growth. In this way, we sought to show what a theologian and pastor can do together, giving the reader new insights into the tradition as well as tools for living the Christian life.

The reader will notice that in each chapter we pick a point of entry and then work our way out, allowing the process of exploring particular doctrines to expand beyond the specific subject. For example, the chapter on creation, while providing biblical interpretation as well as brief descriptions of modernity and postmodernity, becomes an opportunity to examine how we know things, and upon what basis we can believe. The chapter on Christology moves from the theoretical to the concrete, giving Shannon a chance to explain the beauty and value of systematic theology for Christians, while Shawnthea describes how a particular Christology can inform and shape a community of faith. Concerning sin, Shannon begins by exploring some of the differences between Roman Catholic, Reformed, and liberation approaches to the doctrine. But then the discussion shifts, and we argue for a new approach to the doctrine of sin, which becomes the foundation for Shawnthea's sermon. In chapter 4, Shawnthea—for whom the church is central—explores ecclesiology from a pastoral perspective using the theology of Karl Barth. Shannon follows with a description of constructive theology, introducing the field of performance studies, and then offers a reflection on "performing" church. In the last chapter we come closest to a conversation, with both theologian and pastor wrestling with actual questions about heaven. Yet even then, while our discussion touches on issues of time and eternity, embodiment and community, the real value of the chapter is that it shows how one can tease out theological issues at stake in specific questions posed by particular Christians.

In the course of writing this book, there were times this expansive approach was painful, for there is always more to be said. Shannon winces at the brief engagements with doctrines and the quick typologies. Shawnthea has a file filled with essay and sermon material that was excised from the original draft. And there is a list of doctrines and issues that we wanted to explore but could not because we simply ran out of room. Furthermore, by its very nature, this kind of collaboration is a hybrid sort of business, fitting neatly into none of the standard forms of writing on these topics. For all the regrets this causes us, we hope its benefits are greater still, and that somewhere in these pages the reader finds ideas to ponder, argue with, or reject with articulate passion—or that lead to new questions entirely.

We hope that at the end of this book you will find that we did what we set out to do: make a strong case for why theologians and pastors should seek each other out and be in conversation. And while this book may not be a transcript of our own lively conversations, it captures precisely how we engage and influence one another around specific doctrines and broader ideas. We know it's not an easy thing to do, for pastors and theologians speak in different ways, serve different constituencies, and work in different environments. Yet if we can bridge the gap and bring ourselves into closer communion, the results have the power to challenge and transform the way pastors do ministry and the way professors do theology.

Notes

Preface

1. Rosemary P. Carbine, "Ekklesial Work: Toward a Feminist Public Theology," *Harvard Theological Review* 99, no. 4 (October 2006): 433–55.

Chapter 1. Creation

1. They are also about the separation of church and state, but that is a different essay.
2. Note that there are many other resources for a doctrine of creation throughout the Bible.
3. Anne M. Clifford, "Creation," in *Systematic Theology: Roman Catholic Perspectives*, ed. Francis Schüssler Fiorenza and John P. Galvin (Minneapolis: Fortress Press, 1991), 199.
4. For a great take on this, see Rosemary Radford Ruether, *Gaia and God: An Ecofeminist Theology of Earth Healing* (San Francisco: HarperSanFrancisco, 1992), 16ff.
5. Ibid., 17.
6. Clifford, "Creation," 199.
7. Ibid., 200.
8. Ibid., 201–2.
9. Frei is most interested in typological, or figural, readings in relationship to literal readings of the Bible. It is important to note that he

charts a change in what is meant by "literal" reading. See Hans Frei, *The Eclipse of Biblical Narrative: A Study in Eighteenth and Nineteenth Century Hermeneutics* (New Haven: Yale University Press, 1974), 6–7.

10. Ibid., 5.

11. The bacterial flagellum is a favorite example. See Michael J. Behe, *Darwin's Black Box: The Biochemical Challenge to Evolution* (New York: Free Press, 1996).

12. Here I focus on one particular characteristic of modernity. By no means is the desire for certainty the only mark of modern thought. Rather, it is one aspect of the modern worldview that pertains to the current debates regarding creationism.

13. René Descartes, *Discourse on Method and Related Writings*, trans. Desmond M. Clarke (New York: Penguin, 1999), 14.

14. Ibid., 25.

15. I have written about this in more detail and in relation to postmodern analysis of the onto-theo-logic of modernity in Shannon Craigo-Snell, *Silence, Love, and Death: Saying "Yes" to God in the Theology of Karl Rahner* (Milwaukee: Marquette University Press, 2008), 157–60.

16. For example, see Richard Dawkins, "Viruses of the Mind," *Dennett and His Critics: Demystifying Mind*, ed. Bo Dahlbom (Oxford: Blackwell, 1993), 13–27.

17. As such, it is a parasitic discourse, not simply the next thing that happens after modernity. If sexism ended tomorrow, feminism would as well—it would no longer be necessary. Similarly, if modernity ended tomorrow, postmodernity would too.

18. This resonates with Calvinist discussions of sin, although in postmodernism, culture not only impedes but also enables knowledge. Note also that this critique of our knowledge of what is "natural" is fairly devastating for the entire project of natural theology. A firm appreciation for how much our social location shapes our view of the world makes it difficult to imagine reading a vision of God off the creation.

Chapter 2. Christ

1. Elizabeth A. Livingstone, ed., *The Concise Oxford Dictionary of the Christian Church* (Oxford: Oxford University Press, 1977), 99.

2. Cited in Walter Lowe, "Christ and Salvation," *Christian Theology: An Introduction to Its Traditions and Tasks*, ed. Peter C. Hodgson and Robert H. King, rev. ed. (Minneapolis: Fortress Press, 1994), 226.

3. Donald K. McKim, *Westminster Dictionary of Theological Terms* (Louisville: Westminster John Knox, 1996).

4. Delores S. Williams, *Sisters in the Wilderness: The Challenge of Womanist God-Talk* (Maryknoll, N.Y.: Orbis, 1993), 162.

5. Livingstone, *Concise Oxford Dictionary*, 23–24.

6. Serene Jones and Paul Lakeland, eds., *Constructive Theology: A Contemporary Approach to Classical Themes* (Minneapolis: Fortress Press, 2005), 170.

7. Ibid., 171.

8. Ibid.

9. See Williams, *Sisters in the Wilderness*, 164.

10. Ibid., 81.

11. Ibid., 162.

12. Clifford Geertz, *The Interpretation of Cultures: Selected Essays* (New York: Basic, 1973), 93–95, 123.

13. Williams, *Sisters in the Wilderness*, 166.

14. Ibid., 167.

15. Ibid., 164.

16. Emilie M. Townes, ed., *A Troubling in My Soul: Womanist Perspectives on Evil and Suffering* (Maryknoll, N.Y.: Orbis, 1993), 122.

17. Ibid., 120.

18. Ibid., 124.

19. JoAnne M. Terrell, *Power in the Blood? The Cross in the African American Experience* (Maryknoll, N.Y.: Orbis, 1998).

20. For insight into the use of tradition in theology, see Letty M. Russell, *Human Liberation in a Feminist Perspective—A Theology* (Philadelphia: Westminster, 1974), 74ff.

21. Note that while the historical models Shannon summarizes can be mapped on to the timeline framework, there is not a one-to-one correspondence. Those who hold a moral exemplar form of theology locate salvation in the life and ministry of Jesus Christ. Similarly, some who hold a Christus Victor Christology might locate salvation in the resurrection. Yet there may be many other models, not included in Shannon's sampling, that also locate salvation in the resurrection.

22. Caroline M. Noel, "At the Name of Jesus," music by Ralph Vaughn Williams, ed. Percy Dearmer, et. al., music ed. Ralph Vaughn Williams. 2nd ed. (London: Oxford University Press, 1933) Hymn 368.

23. This is a Protestant understanding of the sacraments, which is my tradition.

24. United Church of Christ, *Book of Worship: The United Church of Christ* (New York: United Church of Christ Office for Church Life and Leadership, 1986), 135–36.

25. Inter-Lutheran Commission on Worship, *Lutheran Book of Worship* (Minneapolis: Augsburg, 1978), 122.

26. Ibid., 48.

Chapter 3. Sin

1. See, for example, John Locke, *The Reasonableness of Christianity with A Discourse of Miracles and Part of A Third Letter Concerning Toleration*, ed. I. T. Ramsey (Stanford: Stanford University Press, 1958), 25ff.

2. See Robert Williams, "Sin and Evil," in *Christian Theology: An Introduction to Its Traditions and Tasks*, ed. Peter C. Hodgson and Robert H. King, rev. ed. (Minneapolis: Fortress Press, 1994), 197.

3. Darby Kathleen Ray et al., "Sin and Evil," in *Constructive Theology: A Contemporary Approach to Classical Themes*, ed. Serene Jones and Paul Lakeland (Minneapolis: Fortress Press, 2005), 128–29; Elizabeth A. Livingstone, ed., *The Concise Oxford Dictionary of the Christian Church* (Oxford: Oxford University Press, 1977), 318.

4. Augustine, *On Free Choice of the Will*, trans. A. S. Benjamin and L. H. Hackstaff (Indianapolis: Bobbs-Merrill, 1964), 82–83.

5. Williams, "Sin and Evil," 202.

6. Benjamin Franklin, *Poor Richard's Almanac* (1757).

7. Augustine, "On Grace and Free Will," in *Saint Augustine: Anti-Pelagian Writings*, ed. P. Schaff (Nicene and Post-Nicene Fathers of the Christian Church, vol. 5, 1886; repr., Grand Rapids: Eerdmans, 1978), 456.

8. Ray et al., "Sin and Evil," 134–35.

9. Also, any similarities between contemporary American understandings of alcoholism and Christian theology are neither random nor accidental. Bill W. and Dr. Bob, two of the founders of Alcoholics Anonymous, knew a good bit of Christian theology. The Twelve Steps of AA are a spiritual, not necessarily Christian, program, but due to their heritage they follow some of the dynamics of a Christian theology of sin and grace.

10. The contrast between the two paradigms (nature-grace and sin-redemption) is also a generalization, and one that does not hold up before the modern era even as a general view.

11. Throughout my description of a Roman Catholic view of sin, I will use the twentieth-century theologian Karl Rahner as my primary influence.

12. I am grateful to Ludger Viefhues for his articulation of this relationship.

13. Karl Rahner, *Foundations of Christian Faith: An Introduction to the Idea of Christianity*, trans. William V. Dych (New York: Crossroad, 1982), 111.

14. Karl Rahner, "The Sin of Adam," in *Theological Investigations*, vol. 11, trans. David Bourke (New York: Crossroad, 1974).

15. Again I note that the distinction between act and state is a generalized typology. Rahner and other Roman Catholic theologians also describe the state of fallen humanity, while certainly Reformed Protestants also speak of acts as sinful. For Rahner on the state of fallen nature, see "Brief Theological Observations on the 'State' of Fallen Nature," in *Theological Investigations*, vol. 19, trans. Edward Quinn (New York: Crossroad, 1983).

16. Martin Luther, "A Letter from Luther to Melanchthon," Letter no. 99, August 1, 1521. Dr. Martin Luther's *Saemmtliche Schriften*, vol. 15, ed. Johann G. Walch, trans. Grika Bullmann Flores (St. Louis: Concordia, N.D.) cols. 2585-2590.

17. See Lutheran World Federation and the Catholic Church, *Joint Declaration on the Doctrine of Justification* (Grand Rapids: Eerdmans, 2000).

18. Phillip Berryman, *Liberation Theology: Essential Facts about the Revolutionary Movement in Latin America—and Beyond* (Philadelphia: Temple University Press, 1987), 4, 5. This is an excellent historical and theological introduction to liberation theology, particularly in Latin America.

19. See Gustavo Gutiérrez, *A Theology of Liberation: History, Politics, and Salvation*, trans. and ed. Caridad Inda and John Eagleson (Maryknoll, N.Y.: Orbis, 1973).

20. See Letty M. Russell, *Human Liberation in a Feminist Perspective—A Theology* (Philadelphia: Westminster, 1974).

21. Barbara Kingsolver, *Animal Dreams* (New York: HarperCollins, 1990), 299.

22. For a more thorough exegetical analysis of homosexuality in Scripture, I would commend chapter 8 of Peter J. Gomes, *The Good Book: Reading the Bible with Mind and Heart* (New York: William Morrow, 1996), or part 2 of Walter Wink, ed., *Homosexuality and Christian Faith: Questions of Conscience for the Churches* (Minneapolis: Fortress Press, 1999).

Chapter 4. Church

1. Karl Barth, *Church Dogmatics*, vol. IV.i, trans. G. W. Bromiley (Edinburgh: T. & T. Clark, 1992), 650–725.

2. Actually, the marks of the church were added to the original 325 creed at the Council of Constantinople in 381. Henry Bettenson and Chris Maunder, eds., *Documents of the Christian Church* (Oxford: Oxford University Press, 1999), 28–29.

3. Barth, *Church Dogmatics*, IV.i:676–77, excursus.

4. Alister E. McGrath, *Christian Theology: An Introduction* (Oxford: Blackwell, 1994), 483.

5. Barth, *Church Dogmatics*, IV.i:669.

6. Ibid., 678.

7. Ibid., 690.

8. Ibid., 698.

9. Ibid., 703.

10. Ibid., 709.

11. Ibid., 714.

12. Ibid., 715.

13. Ibid., 736.

14. Ibid.

15. See Marvin Carlson, *Performance: A Critical Introduction*, 2nd ed. (New York: Routledge, 2004), 9–80.

16. For a more detailed description, see Shannon Craigo-Snell, "Theology as Performance," *The Ecumenist* 45, no. 2 (2008): 6–10.

17. Carlson, *Performance*, 5. Here Carlson is summarizing a point made by Richard Baumann, "Performance," in *International Encyclopedia of Communication*, ed. Erik Barnouw (New York: Oxford University Press, 1989).

18. See Richard Schechner, *Performance Studies: An Introduction* (New York: Routledge, 2002), 30, 32.

19. Ibid., 1, 24.

20. Carlson, *Performance*, 13.

21. For an extended analysis of performance of social roles, see Erving Goffman, *The Presentation of Self in Everyday Life* (New York: Anchor, 1959).

22. The work of Peter Brook has been used by a number of theologians, including Timothy Gorringe, *God's Theatre: Theology of Providence* (London: SCM, 1991); and Kevin J. Vanhoozer, *The Drama of Doctrine: A Canonical Linguistic Approach to Christian Theology* (Louisville: Westminster John Knox, 2005). See also Trevor A. Hart and Steven R. Guthrie, eds., *Faithful Performances: Enacting Christian Tradition* (Burlington, Vt.: Ashgate, 2007).

23. Peter Brook, *The Empty Space*, 1st American ed. (New York: Atheneum, 1968), 9.

24. Ibid., 10.

25. Ibid., 33.

26. Ibid., 29.

27. Ibid., 22.

28. Ibid., 15.

29. Ibid., 12.

30. Ibid., 16.

31. Ibid., 42.

32. Ibid.

33. Ibid., 43–44.

34. Ibid., 44.

35. Ibid., 56.

36. Ibid., 47.

37. Ibid., 52.

38. Ibid., 63.

39. Ibid., 46.

40. Ibid., 65.

41. Ibid., 69.

42. Ibid., 71.

43. Ibid., 70.

44. Ibid., 85.

45. Vanhoozer's use of theater in constructive ecclesiology is quite different from what I so briefly suggest in this chapter. Here we specifically disagree, as Vanhoozer does not describe the Rough Theatre and identifies the Immediate Theatre as Brook's preference. Vanhoozer, *Drama of Doctrine*, 406. Joshua Edelman, while noting Vanhoozer's neglect of the Rough Theatre, likewise identifies the Immediate Theatre as Brook's goal. Joshua Edelman, "Can an Act Be True? The Possibilities of the Dramatic Metaphor for Theology within a Post-Stanislavskian Theatre," in Hart and Guthrie, *Faithful Performances*, 52.

46. Brook, *Empty Space*, 96.

47. Ibid., 62.

48. Ibid., 87.

49. Ibid., 133.

50. Ibid., 138.

51. Ibid.

52. Ibid., 139.

53. Ibid.

54. Ibid., 140.

55. Ibid., 134.

56. For a snapshot of some of these discussions, see Thomas C. Reeves, *The Empty Church: The Suicide of Liberal Christianity* (New York: Free Press, 1996); and Robin Gill, *The "Empty" Church Revisited* (Burlington, Vt.: Ashgate, 2003).

57. Karl Barth, *The Epistle to the Romans*, trans. Edwin C. Hoskyns (London: Oxford University Press, 1968), 36.

58. Ibid. Also, Vanhoozer notes that John Webster describes the church as an empty space. Vanhoozer, *Drama of Doctrine*, 435; John Webster, *Word and Church: Essays in Christian Dogmatics* (Edinburgh: T. & T. Clark, 2001), 226.

Chapter 5. Heaven

1. See Irving G. Leon, "Adoption Losses: Naturally Occurring or Socially Constructed?" *Child Development* 73, no. 2 (March–April 2002): 652–63.

2. For theological reflection on this, see Karl Rahner, "The Body in the Order of Salvation," in *Theological Investigations*, vol. 17, trans. Margaret Kohl (London: Darton, Longman & Todd), 87–88.

3. John 6:40.

4. See also Shannon Craigo-Snell, *Silence, Love, and Death: Saying "Yes" to God in the Theology of Karl Rahner* (Milwaukee: Marquette University Press, 2008).

5. See Letty M. Russell, *Human Liberation in a Feminist Perspective—A Theology* (Philadelphia: Westminster, 1974), 72.

6. Ibid., 42ff.

7. Karl Rahner, "Christian Humanism," in *Theological Investigations*, vol. 9, trans. Graham Harrison (London: Darton, Longman & Todd, 1972), 201; Karl Rahner, *Foundations of Christian Faith: An Introduction to the Idea of Christianity*, trans. William V. Dych (New York: Crossroad, 1982), 439.

8. Marilyn McCord Adams defines horrendous evils as "evils, the participation in which (that is, the doing or suffering of which) constitutes prima facie reason to doubt whether the participant's life could (given their inclusion in it) be a great good to him/her on the whole." Marilyn M. Adams, *Horrendous Evils and the Goodness of God* (Ithaca, N.Y.: Cornell University Press, 1999), 26.

9. Tirzah Enumah, "Overruled" (submitted for Christian Understandings of Evil and the Power of God, Yale University, 2002), 17.

10. Revelation 21:4.

11. Miroslav Volf, *The End of Memory: Remembering Rightly in a Violent World* (Grand Rapids: Eerdmans, 2006).

12. See Adams, *Horrendous Evils*, 26.

13. Charles Wesley, "Love Divine, All Loves Excelling," music by John Zundel. *The Chalice Hymnal* (St. Louis, Mo.: Chalice Press, 1995) Hymn 517.

14. Karl Rahner, "The Intermediate State," in *Theological Investigations*, vol. 17, trans. Margaret Kohl (London: Darton, Longman & Todd, 1981), 119, 120.

Bibliography

Adams, Marilyn M. *Horrendous Evils and the Goodness of God*. Ithaca, N.Y.: Cornell University Press, 1999.

Augustine. *On Free Choice of the Will*. Translated by A. S. Benjamin and L. H. Hackstaff. Indianapolis: Bobbs-Merrill, 1964.

———. "On Grace and Free Will." In *Saint Augustine: Anti-Pelagian Writings*, edited by P. Schaff. Nicene and Post-Nicene Fathers of the Christian Church, vol. 5, 1886; repr. Grand Rapids: Eerdmans, 1978.

Barth, Karl. *Church Dogmatics*. Vol. IV.i. Translated by G. W. Bromiley. Edinburgh: T. & T. Clark, 1992.

———. *The Epistle to the Romans*. Translated by Edwin C. Hoskyns. London: Oxford University Press, 1968.

Berryman, Phillip. *Liberation Theology: Essential Facts about the Revolutionary Movement in Latin America—and Beyond*. Philadelphia: Temple University Press, 1987.

Bettenson, Henry, and Chris Maunder, eds. *Documents of the Christian Church*. Oxford: Oxford University Press, 1999.

Brook, Peter. *The Empty Space*. 1st American ed. New York: Atheneum, 1968.

Carbine, Rosemary P. "Ekklesial Work: Toward a Feminist Public Theology." *Harvard Theological Review* 99, no. 4 (October 2006): 433–55.

Carlson, Marvin. *Performance: A Critical Introduction*. 2nd ed. New York: Routledge, 2004.

Clifford, Anne M. "Creation." In *Systematic Theology: Roman Catholic Perspectives*, edited by Francis Schüssler Fiorenza and John P. Galvin. Minneapolis: Fortress Press, 1991.

Craigo-Snell, Shannon. *Silence, Love, and Death: Saying "Yes" to God in the Theology of Karl Rahner*. Milwaukee: Marquette University Press, 2008.

———. "Theology as Performance." *The Ecumenist* 45, no. 2 (2008): 6–10.

Dawkins, Richard. "Viruses of the Mind." In *Dennett and His Critics: Demystifying Mind,* edited by Bo Dahlbom. Oxford: Blackwell, 1993.

Descartes, René. *Discourse on Method and Related Writings*. Translated by Desmond M. Clarke. New York: Penguin, 1999.

Frei, Hans. *The Eclipse of Biblical Narrative: A Study in Eighteenth and Nineteenth Century Hermeneutics*. New Haven: Yale University Press, 1974.

Goffman, Erving. *The Presentation of Self in Everyday Life*. New York: Anchor, 1959.

Gill, Robin. *The "Empty" Church Revisited*. Burlington, Vt.: Ashgate, 2003.

Gomes, Peter J. *The Good Book: Reading the Bible with Mind and Heart*. New York: William Morrow, 1996.

Gutiérrez, Gustavo. *A Theology of Liberation: History, Politics, and Salvation*. Translated and edited by Caridad Inda and John Eagleson. Maryknoll, N.Y.: Orbis, 1973.

Hart, Trevor A., and Steven R. Guthrie, eds. *Faithful Performances: Enacting Christian Tradition*. Burlington, Vt.: Ashgate, 2007.

Kingsolver, Barbara. *Animal Dreams*. New York: HarperCollins, 1990.

Locke, John. *The Reasonableness of Christianity with A Discourse of Miracles and part of A Third Letter Concerning Toleration*. Edited by I.T. Ramsey. Stanford: Stanford University Press, 1958.

Lutheran World Federation and the Catholic Church. *Joint Declaration on the Doctrine of Justification*. Grand Rapids: Eerdmans, 2000.

Rahner, Karl. "The Body in the Order of Salvation." In *Theological Investigations*. Vol. 17. Translated by Margaret Kohl. London: Darton, Longman & Todd, 1981.

———. "Brief Theological Observations on the 'State' of Fallen Nature." In *Theological Investigations*. Vol. 19. Translated by Edward Quinn. New York: Crossroad, 1983.

———. "Christian Humanism." In *Theological Investigations*. Vol. 9. Translated by Graham Harrison. London: Darton, Longman & Todd, 1972.

———. *Foundations of Christian Faith: An Introduction to the Idea of Christianity*. Translated by William V. Dych. New York: Crossroad, 1982.

———. "The Intermediate State." In *Theological Investigations*. Vol. 17. Translated by Margaret Kohl. London: Darton, Longman & Todd, 1981.

———. "The Sin of Adam." In *Theological Investigations*. Vol. 11. Translated by David Bourke. New York: Crossroad, 1974.

Ray, Darby Kathleen, Margaret D. Kamitsuka, Kris Kvam, Sallie McFague, Linda Mercadante, Stephen G. Ray, John E. Thiel, and Tatha Wiley. "Sin and Evil." In *Constructive Theology: A Contemporary Approach to Classical Themes*, edited by Serene Jones and Paul Lakeland. Minneapolis: Fortress Press, 2005.

Ray, Stephen G., Jr. *Do No Harm: Social Sin and Christian Responsibility*. Minneapolis: Fortress Press, 2003.

Reeves, Thomas C. *The Empty Church: The Suicide of Liberal Christianity*. New York: Free Press, 1996.

Ruether, Rosemary Radford. *Gaia and God: An Ecofeminist Theology of Earth Healing*. San Francisco: HarperSanFrancisco, 1992.

Russell, Letty M. *Human Liberation in a Feminist Perspective—A Theology*. Philadelphia: Westminster, 1974.

Schechner, Richard. *Performance Studies: An Introduction*. New York: Routledge, 2002.

Vanhoozer, Kevin J. *The Drama of Doctrine: A Canonical Linguistic Approach to Christian Theology.* Louisville: Westminster John Knox, 2005.

Volf, Miroslav. *The End of Memory: Remembering Rightly in a Violent World.* Grand Rapids: Eerdmans, 2006.

Webster, John. *Word and Church: Essays in Christian Dogmatics.* Edinburgh: T. & T. Clark, 2001.

Williams, Robert. "Sin and Evil." In *Christian Theology: An Introduction to Its Traditions and Tasks,* edited by Peter C. Hodgson and Robert H. King. Rev. ed. Minneapolis: Fortress Press, 1994.

Wink, Walter, ed. *Homosexuality and Christian Faith: Questions of Conscience for the Churches.* Minneapolis: Fortress Press, 1999.

Index